THE THOUGHT LEADERSHIP MANUAL

How to grab your clients' attention with powerful ideas

TIM PRIZEMAN

The Thought Leadership Manual

First published in 2015 by

Panoma Press Ltd
48 St Vincent Drive, St Albans, Herts, AL1 5SJ, UK
info@panomapress.com
www.panomapress.com

Book layout by Neil Coe. Charts by Steven Prizeman.

Printed on acid-free paper from managed forests.

ISBN 978-1-909623-80-4

The right of Tim Prizeman to be identified as the author of this work has been asserted in accordance with sections 77 and 78 of the Copyright Designs and Patents Act 1988.

A CIP catalogue record for this book is available from the British Library.

This book is available online and in bookstores.

Dedication:

This book is dedicated to the memory of Joan Prizeman.

Contents

An introduction from the author

The idea that you need to demonstrate your expertise with important insights, not simply by asserting it in brochures and webpages, has become labelled 'thought leadership' over the past decade or so.

In fact it has become one of the most important elements in the marketing of high-value business services.

Yet it rarely features in marketing courses, while books on the subject have only recently started to appear.

There are, however, countless books and articles borrowing the term that promise to explain how you can 'blog your way to being a thought leader', 'speak your way to being a thought leader' or similar. But all the ones I have seen have a big hole at the centre.

It can be caricatured as 'first you will need to generate a supply of really great ideas... once you have these, do the following to Tweet your way to being a thought leader'.

Of course, having the stream of great ideas is the tough part. Yet this is the part where there is the least advice given.

On top of that, sales success for most established businesses comes from effectively deploying a range of techniques (not just one) and normally from focusing on existing relationships, not from just trying to find and convert new prospects (the toughest sales prospect to crack).

This book fills that gap, and whether you are new to thought leadership or have plenty of experience, it specifically helps you create a successful campaign through:

- Getting it off the ground through successfully getting internal buy-in from colleagues and budget holders.

- Taking you through, in detail, my process that will help you create the all-important great ideas and, essentially, help you identify ideas you think are great but actually aren't.

- Helping you plan and execute a campaign that will deliver the maximum impact in terms of marketing, publicity and, most importantly, sales.

In creating this book I have interviewed numerous knowledgeable people and drawn heavily on over 20 years of personally being involved in such campaigns. Over the years many of these projects have gone well, in fact many have gone really well. The lessons from both the successes and the 'difficult cases' are built into the approach so you don't have to learn them the hard way!

The methodology in this book includes the approach I have developed for Kelso Consulting, my PR and thought leadership agency, and regularly gets applied on successful projects for our clients.

I hope this book proves to be a useful toolkit for you too, bringing you and your business great success.

Yours sincerely

Tim Prizeman, author

Start here

This book is all about growing your business by creating powerful ideas that will grab the attention of clients, prospects and referrers.

Undertaking this sort of activity is often called 'thought leadership' – aiming to turn the person or business into a 'thought leader': a knowledgeable and influential person whom clients trust and turn to for advice – a very powerful position to be in.

We'll be looking at how people have grown businesses and propelled their careers forward, not to mention attracted huge sales, using the techniques outlined in this book.

This book will be showing you the process by which you can achieve this too, taking you through creating great ideas and achieving the biggest possible impact.

This is not an academic book; it is a manual, a workbook that gives you a step-by-step process for achieving great results – ideas that will capture the attention of clients and prospects.

We'll be covering how to create great ideas and get the maximum marketing impact. But more than that, many businesses overlook the leadership aspects. We'll be showing you how you can put your firm, whatever its size, in a true leadership position.

While the term thought leadership is relatively new, creating interesting insights and using them as a tool for commercial benefit is not. Many businesses have been doing it for decades: for instance, the *McKinsey Quarterly* (the main thought leadership vehicle for this famous strategy consultancy) has been running since 1964.

In fact, there are thought leaders throughout history: Adam Smith, for example, whose hugely influential insights on economics were recorded in his classic 18th-century work *The Wealth of Nations*. Promoted through a European speaking tour and other publicity activity at the time, no doubt he would have been an active blogger too if such technology had been around then!

Perhaps you have not been involved in a thought leadership programme before, or maybe you have been involved in such projects elsewhere and want to instigate the benefits of such activity for your new firm.

If so, the first sections of this book are very much for you as they are particularly aimed at people who want to learn more about what thought leadership is, why there is a compelling need for their firm to do it, and the benefits it can bring them and their business.

Alternatively, maybe you are reading this book because you are already involved in such a project and want tips you can implement quickly. If so, this book has hugely useful advice throughout to help you ensure that your current projects are as successful as possible.

By the end of this book you will be in the strongest possible position to propel your firm, and your career, to new success with successful thought leadership initiatives that bring clients, coverage and hopefully the odd accolade too!

SECTION I
USING THOUGHT LEADERSHIP FOR COMPETITIVE ADVANTAGE

CHAPTER 1

Thought leadership: why it is critical for your business

What is thought leadership?

Throughout much of this book I use the term 'thought leadership', one that is widely used (and abused) in the business world. In fact, when writing this book I found there were a whopping 1.74 million pages indexed on Google containing this term.

But what does it mean?

Thought leadership is all about understanding the big trends that are affecting your customers, and being known for it through having demonstrated this expertise by creating attention-grabbing insights.

For instance, law firms are known for having lots of legal experts, accountancy firms have accounting experts and technology firms have IT experts and software with whizzy functions. Much of their marketing simply reinforces this point (when it is never in doubt with your prospects).

Thought leadership, by contrast, is about going beyond promoting yourself as a technical wizard in your particular profession (which you may well be – but so are your many competitors). It is about developing insights on the impact and implications of important matters affecting clients, stakeholders and opinion formers, and sharing them.

The definition I like to use for thought leadership is:

- Original ideas
- With important implications
- Backed by evidence
- Clearly expressed
- Publicly discussed
- That strongly influence the opinions of others

There are other definitions around, but I devised this to highlight the range of things you need to achieve – especially the need for original thought around matters of importance; the need for evidence for your views; and the need to create and communicate insights that influence through their strength and clarity.

Global consultancy Accenture is well known for its thought leadership, which it sees as fundamental to its position as an industry leader. Peter Thomas, its UK head of marketing, described it this way when I interviewed him: "If you want the market to talk about you, talk about the market."

It is a great expression to remember – don't talk about how wonderful your knowledge is, demonstrate it.

And you don't have to be a global gorilla like Accenture to create great thought leadership – lots of small firms on limited budgets are highly successful. This book is very much for people in this position too.

We'll look a bit more at what is and isn't thought leadership later in the book, but for now let's stick with it being about having a strong and interesting point of view, backed by evidence, on a matter that is, or should be, of importance to your clients, and sharing it.

If you can regularly get your clients and contacts thinking *Wow, that's really interesting! I didn't know that, we should look into it further,* then you are a thought leader to them.

What thought leadership means to one of the world's top law firms

Clifford Chance is an international law firm headquartered in London and one of the world's largest.

Thought leadership in recent years has become central to many aspects of its development, marketing and even its culture.

It is overseen at Clifford Chance by its Thought Leadership Board of active thought leaders and other senior figures, which encourages its development and helps focus thought leadership activity on themes important to the whole firm.

Clifford Chance describes thought leadership in its internal documents as something that *comprises views expressed by Clifford Chance that:*

- *are forward looking*
- *contain intellectual content*
- *progress the discussion on a given issue*
- *show a different angle on an existing theme or make new connections*
- *have a cross-border, practice or sector element*

Why is thought leadership important to Clifford Chance? It helps us to:

- *build our brand as intellectual heavyweights, able to lead the debates that are critical to our clients*
- *broker new relationships with our clients – for example, with new parts of their organisation*

- *exercise our influence for the benefit of our clients*

It is a great explanation for the firm's lawyers and support teams that is highly relevant to the firm's market position. Notably, despite being a top commercial law firm, neither the word 'law' nor 'legal' feature in Clifford Chance's definition.

Thought leadership – why do it?

Why should you and your business invest a lot of time and resources producing insights into trends and opportunities that will grab the attention of your clients – the sort of activity often referred to as thought leadership?

After all, it involves time and money. Why not spend this time selling your products or services in sales meetings, with promotional emails, by phone and through whatever other channels you use?

There are lots of reasons, and the rest of this chapter considers them.

I can summarise them as: "*If you and your firm are not well known for being able to tackle the major challenges currently facing your clients, you are in a poor position. If you are up against someone who does, you will probably fail.*"

We all know that many aspects of the business world we face are like the staircases at Hogwarts in the Harry Potter books: they change rapidly and unpredictably, taking us to uncertain destinations.

Your business needs people thinking about what all this means – both for your own business and also for your clients.

Businesses with insights into these challenges that grab the interest of executives will always find themselves in a more powerful position than competitors who lack them.

Many businesses (and professionals) are already doing this, and those that do it well have achieved success – often stunning success.

Why thought leadership is important for your firm

1 – The need to differentiate

Here is the bad news...

To the outside world your firm probably appears pretty similar to your competitors.

For instance, the thousands of accountancy firms. They offer the same sorts of services: audit, tax, general business advice, personal finance and maybe corporate finance, insolvency and forensic.

They employ people with the same qualifications and backgrounds. The firms all use similar software and methodologies for their work, especially in audit, the core service for many firms.

They are all similarly conservative, operate from similar-looking offices and are staffed with professionals who generally look and dress the same. For instance, you won't find many emos, punks or people with visible tattoos doing your audit.

In fact, they have probably worked at other accountancy firms, so not only do they employ similar people, they are the same people moving from one place to fit comfortably into another.

The same applies to law firms, management consultancies, corporate PR agencies and business software companies (well, at least in terms of the people clients meet; the programmers who are hidden from view are a much more motley bunch).

In fact, having great people, great processes, a great looking brand, a snazzy website and competent marketing aren't differentiators at all, these are par for the course.

In a crowded business marketplace, it's very hard to differentiate yourself.

Consequently, it is really hard for clients to distinguish between one firm and another. That makes it hard for them to appreciate why they should use your firm rather than a similar (and perhaps cheaper or larger) one down the road.

So how can you stand out and be memorable?

If you are clearly different from your competitors, it is easy for people to remember you, recommend you and justify (to themselves and colleagues) using you. If you have a strong, clear 'value proposition' (ie how you deliver more value than your competitors) you can win more *and* charge more.

One of the strongest ways of standing out and being chosen is by being known for having strong expertise in particular markets and/ or having expert know-how at solving specific important business challenges.

Sarah Reavley, a partner in research agency Remark, which specialises in working with professional firms, says: "In our 15 years of undertaking client satisfaction research, we have found that industry and sector expertise is consistently listed as a 'top three' selection criteria by most professional firm clients. Anything your firm can do to enhance its reputation as experts is likely to result in increased opportunities for new businesses and greater competitive success."

Let's return to the accountancy sector as an example. There are lots of accountancy firms but very few (besides the largest) have reputations for expertise in particular industry or other market sectors – being known as experts in helping technology entrepreneurs, for instance. Similarly, having a strong reputation for solving major business problems also differentiates firms (eg particular expertise in helping businesses raise capital or export).

However, there are notable exceptions. Mid-sized accountancy firms PKF Littlejohn and Kingston Smith are well recognised for their strength in niche markets – the Lloyd's reinsurance market and London's creative agencies, respectively. Both of them punch well above their weight in these markets, successfully taking on much larger competitors.

Notably, both have been undertaking thought leadership activity for many years to build and protect their position in these markets.

The same applies to businesses in all sorts of advisory, consultancy and business technology markets. Having a strong reputation for expertise makes it easier for people to remember you, to recommend you, and to justify using you to their colleagues.

In fact, if your firm is known as a leading expert in a particular market, you will find yourself automatically being recommended and approached for work, and also invited on to the tenders.

Thought leadership is all about achieving this by building and highlighting particular areas of knowledge where you are strong to ensure that you stand out in the mind of buyers.

Thought leadership is...

- Original ideas
- With important implications
- Backed by evidence
- Clearly expressed
- Publicly discussed
- That strongly influence the opinions of others

Thought leadership – where can it help my business?

If you can say yes to all of the following then you and your business are in a strong position.

If not, then you have important weaknesses that need tackling – thought leadership may well be the answer.

- We understand the important trends affecting our clients' markets and their impact
- We are developing services that reflect our clients' future requirements
- We are well known, by prospects and referrers, for our expertise in important areas
- We are clearly differentiated compared to similar sized competitors, and this is well recognised by the market
- We charge premium rates compared to many competitors
- We regularly win assignments against larger competitors without competing on cost
- We have strong contacts at senior level with our clients and prospects
- At pitches, we get strong feedback on our 'commercial insights'
- Our team has lots of great ideas that we share with our clients and prospects
- We receive a good flow of the 'right' sort of leads in terms of quality of client and project size

2 – Your clients, especially the big ones, expect it

Executives at larger businesses simply expect that their advisers – such as accountants, bankers, technology specialists, consultants and lawyers – will provide value-added services and thought leadership.

They know you are great at whatever your firm does at a technical level. What they want to know is whether you have the vision and knowledge to help them at a strategic level.

As an example, I was recently at a client's sales conference. Their sales team was receiving a presentation from the CIO of a major international travel company on what he wants from his suppliers. He told my client's sales force that their huge and leading-edge cloud and data network infrastructure counted for little as there were numerous competitors now in the market with similar capabilities.

He wanted to know how the customers of his company, who each year across Europe buy millions of holidays, will be selecting and purchasing their holidays in five or 10 years' time, so he is investing now in order to have the right infrastructure in place.

He was very clear. He wants IT suppliers with vision who will help him and his board understand and prepare for this – and, of course, then deliver it.

In short, he wants suppliers that are thought leaders, and he is not the only one.

This point is made strongly, in a different way, by Simon James – a senior litigation partner at global law firm Clifford Chance who has led a number of thought leadership initiatives. He says: "In our markets it is no longer sufficient for us to 'do the deal' and then walk away and await the next instruction. You need to be able to think outside of your narrow technical area and have a sensible discussion with the client on their business challenges. For City lawyers this is a big change."

3 – Thought leadership unlocks high-level sales

Reaching senior executives in large organisations is tough. They are busy people who are frequently in meetings or out and about.

They rarely answer external phone calls, and you have to get past at least one PA to reach them (and often several).

That does not mean they are impossible to reach, nor does it mean they are not interested in thought-provoking ideas from suppliers and would-be suppliers.

Quite the opposite: they are very interested, but their time is precious and they do not want it wasted.

In particular, they typically do not want sales meetings. After all, sifting through salespeople is why they employ a whole legion of people and a procurement department too.

So if you approach CEOs (and other senior executives) with a sales mentality then you typically don't get far as they are rarely in buying mode.

By contrast, undertaking thought leadership is one of the best ways to reach them and get the meeting (and then use it to impress them so you get the all-important result: a second meeting) – by grabbing their attention when you tell them something important that they didn't know.

After all, if you are coming with useful insights that help the CEO deal with some of his biggest challenges, who wouldn't want a second meeting?

Chief executives DO want to meet suppliers, but not time wasters

A small management consultancy in London shared with me their experience of hosting a dinner that was attended by 10 CEOs from FTSE 100 companies (the UK's largest listed businesses). This was a huge achievement, especially as it resulted from a speculative invitation to big businesses they'd had no contact with before.

The subject of the dinner was successful post-merger integration and the speaker was a client and former CEO who had been involved in some big deals, who would share his experiences.

Now, post-merger integration is hardly a new theme, nor was the dinner promising any revolutionary insights. The consultancy was niche and not especially well known.

Why the great response? The invitation had something that CEOs find valuable: the opportunity to hear another CEO's first-hand experience of something that is important to their personal role.

I give the example to illustrate the point that CEOs *are* interested in meetings with suppliers.

They *are* interested in your ideas. They like to go out and about to network, and most of them don't like to be cosseted away in an ivory tower surrounded by 'yes' men.

But you need to convince them that you can share something they will value if you want a slice of their very limited time. This is where most suppliers fail.

4 – To work, much of your marketing needs a flow of ideas

Once upon a time, selling professional and other high-value services was quite straightforward. There was plenty of demand, not too many suppliers and few sources of information. Your network's recommendations, your firm's reputation, and some well-worded ads and brochures would bring enough work.

In the relationship between buyer and seller, the information advantage resided with the seller since they knew their market and product well, while the buyer typically did not. For the buyer, a recommendation from a trusted contact was gold dust as it was the best and often only way to identify a reliable supplier.

This is no longer the case. For most products and services (and, indeed, problems) information is widespread and buyers, whether home owners purchasing holidays and domestic appliances or big corporates buying multimillion-pound investments, do a lot of prior research.

The power of Google means they have immediate access to the latest news, trends, prices and reviews. In fact, they can quickly track down other users and get their experiences. Sellers know their offerings well, but the buyer can quickly re-balance the information advantage with research.

So, we have more and more people searching the internet for advice from experts and suppliers at a very early stage of the buying process (or, perhaps more accurately, the *pre-buying* process). How do you market to these independent and self-directed buyers?

Anyone involved in marketing will not have missed the buzzword 'content marketing' and also the need to feed the hungry mouths of your online marketing channels with Tweets, blogs, videos and podcasts. These activities are designed to attract these prospects while they are searching.

It is quite a task, unless you are brilliant at thinking up blogs and commentary (some people are, but most of us aren't) or have a programme to help create them. This is, of course, where thought leadership fits in.

Having a process that helps you create insights and share them is the missing link in many organisations' marketing, without which their content is flat and the marketing ineffective.

One of my clients refers to the need for a 'thought leadership engine' – a systematic process for creating ideas that form the basis of interesting content. It's quite a term, perhaps a bit American for my liking, but the idea is totally sound.

In fact, many organisations work their marketing 'back to front'. For instance, they decide they need to have a Twitter feed or a monthly newsletter (after all, their competitors do) and they spend their time scratching their heads over what to Tweet and write about.

Better to start with a programme that generates ideas and insights, and then use your marketing channels with the confidence that you have something interesting to shout about.

5 – 'Leading with value' to build relationships before people enter 'buying mode'

As the internet fills up with more and more content, how do you stand out?

While design and visuals are important, it is insights and ideas that matter.

While design and visuals are important, it is insights and ideas that matter.

People may well want to know how wonderful your firm and your services are when they are making a shortlist. But to get on to the shortlist, it takes an effective marketing campaign to identify the prospect, nurture them, influence them, impress them and ensure that you are one of the finalists.

This is particularly difficult for businesses selling very high-value items that need the sign-off of board-level directors – a notoriously hard audience to reach. But it is also a problem faced by businesses of all sizes.

Prospects rarely want to hear about the specifics of products and services until they are ready to buy, but when they *are* ready to buy they have often already made their mind up.

How do you overcome this Catch-22 situation?

Marketing consultant Ian Brodie uses the expression 'leading with value'.

> Don't lead with capabilities, services and other me-too sales messages; most of your targets are not interested until they are in buying mode. Instead 'lead with value' to be memorable and useful to your prospect.

It is all about giving buyers something that they will value – typically some sort of insight or valuable information that will help them with the problem or opportunity they are considering. It is not the same as giving away your product or service for free; it is about giving something that is valuable to the buyer.

Powerful insights and research, case studies, advice, diagnostics and guides all fall into this category. They are great tools to use to get meetings.

They help position you as a source of knowledge and expertise, while helping the buyer with their decision, subtly but firmly positioning you as the sort of firm they can work with.

In fact, not only does this help get you on the pitch, but if you have been using these tools proactively and not waiting for tender invitations, it often helps avoid having to pitch at all.

I think 'leading with value' is a great expression.

6 – Being positioned for the future, not the past

Thought leadership initiatives are generally strongly associated with sales and marketing.

While this is not surprising and not a bad thing per se, what it does mean is that many firms blinker themselves to the wider benefits, looking at them as short-term tactical initiatives rather than longer term strategic ones.

Although it is quite normal for manufacturing and technology businesses to have a research and development team (in fact, who would invest in one that didn't?), there is rarely such a thing in many high-value service businesses like consultancies and law firms.

Thought leadership is all about creating insights into important developments affecting your customers and markets, and this should form a vital part of your own business's planning.

After all, if your customers are going to be demanding more help and solutions in a particular area, you can position yourself for this, creating the necessary services and alliances.

Similarly, if a particular market is emerging or going to struggle, you need to be positioned to identify and seize the opportunities.

I argue strongly that thought leadership activity must not be seen purely as a tactical sales or publicity activity. It is important research into the markets you serve, helping you understand whether and how your firm will be making money in three, five or 10 years' time.

Markets move and change. Your firm can either be at the leading edge or playing catch up.

A good example of this is the rise of the shadow banking market – an emerging, busy and exciting area. But it is both a threat and an opportunity to professional advisers with large banking practices that have served the established financial institutions, not the new ones playing in this sector.

Among others, international law firm Clifford Chance has recognised this (being known for its strong banking expertise) and the firm has ensured that a major focus of its thought leadership activity now covers the shadow banking market. This is both to build its reputation here to capture the best work, but also so it is in touch as this emerging market continues to grow and change.

7 – Thought leadership boosts your career and your 'personal brand'

A really successful career requires you to create demand for yourself – whether from clients, within your own firm or from future employers. Ability is important, but there are lots of able people, so you need to have something of value that is distinctive to you.

Know-how, qualifications and technical expertise are valuable and distinctive, as are contacts and a great track record of success. Lots of people have these too.

Whatever your really strong selling points are, having a great reputation makes you even more valuable. This is sometimes called a 'personal brand'.

Creating a personal brand for yourself and having the skills to build leads and a powerful reputation for your employer is a hugely valuable skill, as is the ability to bring insights of strategic significance to your business and those of your clients.

The broader a canvas you can paint, the greater your ability to perform at the highest levels. However, this does not fit well with many professionals who like the comfort of a narrow technical area.

To see how one partner simultaneously propelled his own career and the profits of his firm, see the following case study of Deloitte's Sports Business Group – an industry-leading practice which initially started in 1992 as three blokes who liked football.

In interviews, both Accenture and Clifford Chance (global leaders in their professions) emphasised how thought leadership is part of the culture. At Accenture it is very much 'in the blood', while at Clifford Chance thought leadership started to fit recognisably into the firm's strategy about five years ago.

Kate Gibbons, the partner with overall responsibility for thought leadership at Clifford Chance, says: "If someone is recognised as an expert and well connected, it benefits the whole firm. If people are talking about your firm then you will get the best instructions and we were keen to encourage our people to position themselves as experts in their areas.

"The holy grail in your legal career is to move from salary to equity partner. At Clifford Chance, to do this you now need to be recognised in your sector, and a new partner is not only required to be a great lawyer, they also must be able to speak well, network well and have a recognised position as an expert in their area."

Accenture's UK head of marketing, Peter Thomas, says: "Historically, having a piece of published content was very much a part of the progression path for your career. It is now not a cast-iron requirement, but still having something in the public domain, with your name on it, will be good for your career.

"We want people who are seen as informed and leading the market and it is a vivid way of you demonstrating that you are adding value to the business. If someone at Accenture had to ask why this is good, then they are probably not the right person for a senior role."

Thought leadership case study – Gerry Boon and Deloitte's Sports Business Group

Gerry Boon is a great example of someone who has used thought leadership to create a fantastic career for himself and stellar success for his firm, Deloitte.

Originally the firm had a smattering of football and sports-related clients spread about its tax and audit teams in a range of offices.

Thanks to a highly successful thought leadership initiative – *The Deloitte Annual Review of Football Finance* – an industry-leading team of two dozen sports business professionals has been created from a starting point of three accountants with an interest in sports finance.

The process was partly driven by necessity. Gerry was originally a partner at mid-tier firm Spicer & Oppenheim, where he balanced fee-earning work (a quarter of his time) with management roles, being in charge of marketing in London and also the firm's national finance partner.

In 1990 he took three months off because his wife was unwell, during which time the firm 'merged' with larger rival Touche Ross (now Deloitte), so he returned to find that he had no position of authority and few clients.

This was a potentially vulnerable position in a cost-conscious firm like Touche, which was about to embark on its own post-merger integration process. So Gerry set himself the challenge of creating a marketing activity that, as he describes it, "ticked the boxes of being good quality, professional, linked to our services, and profile raising. My criteria also included creating something you can measure and track over time, so you can develop stories out of the changes, achieve continuity, and attract and retain a following audience."

He adds: "I was quite PR-savvy by the standards of accountants at the time – you have to remember that we had only been able to advertise since 1986, just four years before.

"One day, looking at football results for my beloved Oldham Athletic, inspiration struck. As accountants, we could be looking at 'financial league tables for football'… it was a eureka moment, or maybe just a glimpse of the blindingly obvious, depending on your perspective."

It was an auspicious time for considering the finance of sport. In 1992 the Premier League was formed, driven by the desire of the clubs in what was then the First Division to take advantage of lucrative television rights from the first deal with Sky. There was also the aftermath of the Taylor report following the Hillsborough stadium disaster, meaning that clubs had three years to get safety certificates, which required finding hundreds of millions of pounds of finance for stadium upgrades.

With the assistance of manager Steve Cummings and tax partner Richard Baldwin, in 1992 Gerry produced the rather staidly named *Survey of Significant Accounting Policies of Football Clubs*, based on 1991 club accounts. He observes that the title was quickly changed (the next year) to the much more eye-catching *Annual Review of Football Finance*, now in its 23rd edition.

Gerry says: "The media lapped it up as people had not previously thought of football clubs as businesses, surprisingly as it may seem today. The timing was brilliant… you need to get lucky, although clearly we knew this was going on, given our work in football with the FA and others."

In addition to PR, the report was distributed to all the football clubs and leagues and as many people as possible who were influential in the sport, including lawyers, bankers and sport governing bodies.

It didn't all go smoothly, but confidence allowed the team to turn a big initial problem to their advantage.

Gerry says: "Within days of the first report appearing, we had a letter from renowned libel law firm Carter-Ruck regarding what we had said about Chelsea's accounts.

"The upshot was we had to amend the report in a couple of places and send a 'correction' letter to all the recipients. It was not a disaster – far from it. Chelsea's then chairman was, shall we say, a polarising figure. As it happened, upsetting him got us a favourable reaction from many in the football sector and, either way, it certainly meant the report was being talked about by the right people.

"As a result of the apology letter going out, we quickly received around 20 business leads! It gave our business a boost, and it was also the first of three occasions when he attempted to take legal action against the firm.

"One of the enquiries led to a conversation with the then financial director of Manchester United, which had just gone on the Stock Exchange and its shares had fallen by over a third from the issue price. He felt the City did not understand it as a business and sought our views. I observed that its accounts did not include its two most valuable assets: the stadium and the playing squad.

"The upshot was that Touche Ross came up with a unique valuation methodology for the squad that had never before been performed. It generated headlines in the *FT* when the club's annual results were published, and I recall its share price went up by around 30%, adding millions to the market capitalisation. A massive return on our fee!

"After this, work started to roll in and within a year we had a credible specialist team in football and were branching into other areas of sport. The amount of work generated by the profile very quickly made it necessary to create a specialist unit, primarily based around people in Manchester, and also specialist stadium consultancy people in St Albans and the London tax team, which Richard Baldwin led.

"Having started as three or four blokes with an interest in the area, by the time I retired in February 2005 there were 18 people full time in Deloitte on sport, and it has grown even more subsequently.

"My career and the football expertise and sports business group became synonymous. I was 37 when this started, and it became a major determinant of my career as, within a year or so, I was working full time on clients, spending on average 10 to 15 hours a week briefing the media. Thereafter the firm's expertise and my own profile became synonymous with football clubs' accounts and sports business consulting.

"I did it for 15 years and retired in 2005. Travelled, met loads of interesting people, and went to loads of places in Europe and farther afield, where one doesn't usually find an 'accountant'.

"It has led to rewarding careers for a large number of our excellent people and has created a massive profile for the firm. It's given Deloitte pre-eminence and leadership in this field for 20 years; made it hard for others to get into this space; given a huge amount of self-esteem for people at Deloitte (as sport is relevant and interesting to the vast majority of people); and is a great recruiting tool for the firm."

Among the reasons why it was successful, Gerry particularly identifies:

1. Getting the 'first mover' advantage.

2. The subject's topicality (and also its longevity – now in its 23rd edition).

3. Using this to grab the space and create the profile, making it hard for others to catch up.

4. Followed up initial initiatives energetically and with good-quality work, building on our existing platform.

5. Being prepared to engage the media regularly and consistently (many professionals hide their light under a bushel).

6. This created a virtuous circle – all of this activity generated more work and my colleagues and I quickly became the recognised experts.

With hindsight it sounds a no-brainer that this would be a good idea. Don't be deceived. Gerry says: "You need to be determined to make it happen. Within the firm there were those very traditional and conservative senior people who were opposed to this activity, particularly the fact it was in 'football' and dealing with the media, and didn't think it was a good idea. I suppose it was my vision as well as the passionate force of my personality that enabled me to counter that!"

Case study – Ian Brodie, marketing adviser to small and self-employed consultants

This book contains examples from big global firms like Accenture, Clifford Chance and Deloitte.

But you absolutely must not draw the conclusion that it is something that only big businesses can do properly. There are also plenty of examples of SMEs that have achieved great success.

Ian Brodie is a case in point, having built a very successful reputation and business as a self-employed marketing consultant using thought leadership in his areas of expertise: coaching other small and self-employed consultants on bringing in more leads and sales. He backs up his ideas with strong email marketing and a website designed to attract visitors and turn them into qualified leads.

Ian says: "When I set up my own business in 2007, I wasn't thinking that I needed to do thought leadership to be successful as an independent consultant, although I was familiar with it, having been involved with it at my previous firm – a very large technology consultancy.

"I'd always been involved with it and always found it rewarding for me and the business.

"When I set up, I did have some ideas I had not seen elsewhere that I wanted to get off my chest.

"My blog was successful and this encouraged me to share more ideas.

"Relatively quickly, sharing ideas paid off, which made me see it as a good thing, and things continued from there.

"The benefits to me have included making it easier for people to find me. When they do find me, whether because of my book, the blog or the podcasts and webinars I do, they already know me. I get a lot of direct clients from this.

"But, better than that, having a high profile and reputation preconditions people to think about me a certain way, which makes it easier to sell. In fact, by the time they approach me they have often made up their mind and are almost ready to buy.

"For instance, if you contrast it with business networking, when you meet someone you don't know, it is a level playing field with everyone else and this favours people who are good at networking.

"I would rather put lots of effort into producing intellectual property so that people already know me and that makes me higher in their estimation. Now, if people meet me and already know about me, they look at me in a different light. I often get people saying: 'It is great to finally meet you.'

"In fact, this does snowball and make it easier for people to recommend you. If you have this recognised position as a thought leader, people get kudos for recommending an expert, as opposed to recommending someone unknown.

"If you have produced lots of great material then that builds a trust angle that makes people more likely to buy – I have certainly experienced this and it has helped my business enormously."

Ian warns that you have to be prepared to think and put in the work to stand out. It is definitely not for everyone. He says: "You've got to do your homework to create new ideas, go in-depth as much as possible, and find a different spin and angle. If you want something to work for you, it's got to have been difficult.

"In terms of how I keep up high levels of output, I have some core ideas and concentrate on new ways of explaining and putting them across."

The best stuff has evolved from Ian's own experiences and putting the work in, including:

- Some deep thought into creating models (Ian has two unique models).

- Ian is thinking about the topic all of the time – that way, ideas come to him, but he still has to work hard on getting the facts.

- One of Ian's areas of expertise is email marketing, and he often runs tests and writes about the results. He talks about the successes, but also the failures – not many people do this. Not only are the failures instructional, but it gives his followers a feel for his authenticity and they know that they aren't getting material from a glossed-over public persona.

Another striking element of Ian's output is the simplicity of the language and the everyday sources of the anecdotes and illustrations his emails and blogs contain – a great approach that has done well for billionaire investor Warren Buffett too!

To experience a great example of thought leadership in action, go to www.ianbrodie.com and sign up to Ian's reports and emails.

CHAPTER 2

Thought leadership: what it means in practice

In Chapter 1 we saw how thought leadership is about having a strong and interesting point of view, backed by evidence, on a matter that is (or should be) of importance to your clients, and then gaining recognition (and commercial advantage) through communicating this.

This chapter is for you if you want to understand the term more and where the term fits with your marketing as well as with buzz words you may come across such as 'content marketing', 'challenger selling', 'go-to person', etc.

What is thought leadership?

Thought leadership is a used and abused business jargon term that covers all manner of approaches to becoming a notable and influential authority. You could also say it is a really exciting way to grow and evolve your business and your career.

To start with, it is probably important to set out how we will use the term. In this book we will talk about:

- Doing thought leadership – that is, creating and publicising insights that will be of interest to your clients.

- Being a thought leader – that is, being widely recognised and rated for your interesting insights and knowledge, and having the credibility to influence others (generally from having **done** a lot of thought leadership to earn this recognition).

Generally, you have to *do a lot of thought leadership* if you are to *become a thought leader*.

However, highly successful business people can become famous and have views that become influential simply through the credibility of their track record (and, of course, they may well benefit from other factors, like charisma and celebrity appeal, too).

Thought leadership = ugly term

In this book, the term 'thought leadership' gets used an awful lot. Quite frankly, it's not a term I particularly like!

It is generally credited as being coined in 1994 by the editor of Booz & Co's *Strategy & Business* journal for particular interviewees. It has become widely popularised, used and abused as a buzz phrase for a person or business recognised as a leader in their sector.

Personally, I don't like the phrase because it can sound both ugly and overblown. It is also sometimes misinterpreted as setting an unrealistically high bar for what firms need to achieve. We aren't talking of insights having to be completely ground-breaking (such fundamental intellectual breakthroughs do not come around that frequently); the aim is simply the creation of new and interesting perspectives that grab the attention of clients and others.

However, the term is useful because it reinforces that you do have to put in a lot of 'thought', and if your thinking produces innovative ideas you can exploit them to gain influence (in other words, some sort of leadership position).

Wikipedia, the online encyclopaedia, has a definition for Thought Leadership that changes regularly due to being continually re-edited. The last time I looked it was:

"Thought leadership is business jargon for an entity that is **recognised** by peers for having **innovative ideas**... Thought leaders often **publish** articles and blog posts on **trends and topics influencing an industry**."

There are some really good bits in this. First of all you have to be recognised for your innovative ideas, and you need to share them by publishing them, and typically your thoughts will be on trends and topics influencing an industry.

BusinessDictionary.com has an alternative definition for Opinion Leaders that I really like:

"Influential members of a community, group or society to whom others turn for advice, opinions and views."

I particularly like this definition for an opinion leader – an influential person to whom others turn for advice, opinions and views. What professional or executive would not want to be such a person?

Besides thought leader and opinion leader, other widely used terms include:

1. Authority Marketing: you gain a marketing advantage by positioning you or your business as an authority on a particular topic.

2. Content Marketing: you have lots of interesting reports, videos or other 'content' online that you use to attract, and nurture relationships with, prospects and clients.

3. Educational Marketing: especially in a new area, you educate and inform people about a problem that you can help them solve.

4. 'Go-To' Person: people recommend and approach you because you have a great reputation for being a networked and informed person in your market or area of expertise.

5. Recognised Specialist /Recognised Expert.

You may come across other terms. If so, do email them to me – I'm always keen to find out more!

In this book we are not going to get too hung up over the esoterics of the difference between thought leadership and, say, authority marketing or whether you would rather be seen as a recognised expert or a thought leader.

We're here to create and exploit ideas that will excite your clients so that you get lots of additional clients and new projects.

If you would rather call that authority marketing, that is fine by me! What we do need to be clear about is that it involves:

- Original ideas
- With important implications
- Backed by evidence
- Clearly expressed
- Publicly discussed
- Strongly influencing the opinions of others

Thought leadership is all around us

In fact, thought leadership is all around us. Whether it is leading business groups announcing monthly business confidence surveys, the debate about global warming, research into Generation Y, the popular notion that your left brain hemisphere is more analytical and your right hemisphere more creative, or all the research that you can see published most days in national newspapers by businesses, academics, charities and political parties seeking to influence our opinions.

Thought leadership can be delivered in all sorts of ways, including:

- Reports
- White papers and articles

- PowerPoint
- Emails
- Books
- Online via webpages, Tweets, LinkedIn, blogs and other social media
- Podcasts and videos
- Via the media
- And, of course, verbally in meetings, interviews, and at other events

What thought leadership isn't

The easiest way to have a Thought Leadership Programme is simply to call the stuff you do already 'thought leadership'!

Lots of firms do this. It is particularly prevalent in the US, where 'thought leadership' and 'PR' are often used almost interchangeably. In fact, I have heard all of the following referred to as thought leadership:

- Brochures
- Sales pitches and product sheets
- Viewpoints with no supporting evidence
- Technical update newsletters (on such things as tax, employment law, building regulations)
- Routine press releases
- Opinion surveys (with no analysis or commentary)
- Recycled content (typically through rehashing other people's ideas, but without giving them any credit)

While I am not saying that some of the above do not have an important part to play in the marketing of professional and other B2B businesses, let's not kid ourselves; they are not thought leadership because either they have no new insights or important implications, or because they are rarely influential in changing the views of others.

CHAPTER 3

What makes a great thought leader?

Some people characterise thought leadership as being all about doing research.

I don't think that is correct, and nor did many of the people I interviewed in the course of writing this book. You certainly need evidence that is credible to support your views, and research can provide this.

However, influential business people and commentators have gained their position of authority through all sorts of ways.

Ten examples include:

1. Hero entrepreneurs and hero managers – examples include Sir Richard Branson, Lord Sugar, Donald Trump, Jack Welch

Hero entrepreneurs are people whose achievements, in this case being highly successful self-made business people, give their views huge credibility.

The most famous (and also the not-so-famous) often use social media to cultivate a fan base, successfully blurring the border between business and celebrity. Lord Sugar (3.5 million followers on Twitter), rehabilitated prisoner Martha Stewart (2.8 million) and Donald Trump (2.7 million) are good examples.

Sir Richard Branson is perhaps the epitome (4.4 million followers on Twitter and a further 6.4 million on LinkedIn, for instance). Many of Sir Richard's followers are more like disciples of his gospel, and no doubt if he posted "wearing red underwear was the secret to my success" sales of it would rocket!

Of course, you don't have to be a billionaire or convicted tax fraudster to make this work for you; it works with people who have simply made themselves multimillionaires too.

John Timpson, the chairman of high street key-cutter and shoe-repairer Timpsons, regularly appears in newspapers and magazines giving great business advice in a characteristically folksy style, as does Peter Hargreaves, financial adviser and co-founder of Hargreaves Lansdown.

Hero managers are their less rock 'n' roll cousins – successful career executives from big companies whose track record (and perhaps also a bit of borrowed kudos from their employer's brand) gives their views strong credibility.

Jack Welch is a great example (also cultivating a fan base on Twitter, with 1.4 million followers) as are Lee Iacocca and the late Sir John Harvey-Jones.

2. The role model

Like the hero entrepreneur, the role model's status comes from achievement – in their case walking the talk in a way that inspires others.

Examples include the late Dame Anita Roddick who was not only a successful entrepreneur, but famously an early innovator in ethical consumerism and fair trade through her Body Shop skin care and bubble bath chain. Bill Gates also aims to be a role model for philanthropy through the Bill & Melinda Gates Foundation.

Financier George Soros falls into this category. Whatever his other achievements, and no matter how widespread his views are reported, he remains first and foremost known for being 'the man who broke the Bank of England' through his lucrative short sale of $10 billion-worth of pounds during 1992's Black Wednesday.

Others in this category include sports stars whose achievements and training discipline give their advice strong credibility and, of course, some celebrity stardust.

Many firms seek to set themselves as role models too, talking about such things as their diversity or green credentials.

The extreme version is The Crusader, determined to reshape the world – whether it wants to be reshaped or not. Apple co-founder and visionary Steve Jobs may well fit this mantle, as do controversial figures such as WikiLeaks founder Julian Assange.

3. The eyewitness

The eyewitness gains authority from having witnessed important events as a fly on the wall or from first-hand involvement, even if it was only a minor role (on the basis of "I was there so I know more than others").

Author Michael Lewis is a great example with his initial book and bestseller *Liar's Poker*. It's a rip-roaring memoir of his short-lived career at bond traders Salomon Brothers and still one of the definitive accounts of the greed that drives the financial markets. It has also positioned him well for a future as an author, columnist and speaker.

Whistle-blowers, such as Sherron Watkins at Enron, also fall into this category when they use this as a launch pad for books, speaking events and perhaps consultancy.

Of course, you don't have to have a bestselling memoir, although it certainly helps as politicians and many others have realised. Case studies take the same principle of documenting your first-hand experience to promote your credentials for helping people facing similar problems.

4. The number cruncher

There is nothing like a statistic or two to bring credibility. A tried and tested way of establishing a thought leadership position is the production of data – whether surveys, usage figures, prices or anything else that can be measured and a trend attached to it.

Academics, City analysts, economists, think-tanks, banks, trade unions, trade associations and, of course, professional firms are just some of the types of organisation issuing reports to gain credibility, recognition and influence. Later on we will look at how you can do this too.

Opinion poll and social trends guru Sir Robert Worcester, the founder of MORI, is a great example, as is the CBI, the trade association for big business. Another is IT security firm Symantec, whose annual Internet Security Threat Report, tracking trends in malware, computer viruses and other IT nasties, is now in its 19th edition.

In fact, anyone can apply this technique thanks to the rise of the internet and Big Data as there is so much out there that can be analysed easily and cheaply.

Later in this book we will look particularly at how you too can use data successfully to add impact and credibility to your thought leadership.

5. The pundit

Pundits are people who regularly give opinion and commentary in the media on subjects where they appear to be knowledgeable. For instance, you can hardly see a news broadcast without some economist speculating about the implications of new or forthcoming data.

The media, especially national newspapers and the main television channels, are hugely influential, so appearing on these regularly gives recognition, influence and credibility.

Many people want to become pundits because it seems an easy shortcut to harnessing the power of the media to grow their business's brand (or, indeed, their own). Often the more you are interviewed, the more credibility you get and consequently the more other journalists want to interview you, and the more... etc.

So how do you do it? It is a circular issue: for the media to view you as someone worth interviewing regularly you need to have a reason for them to consider you – ie what makes you so notable that they should interview you in the first place?

Being a well-recognised expert is typically the way to get the all-important first interview. Other ways include being a pal of the show's producer and being a last-minute stand-in when the first choices have dropped out at short notice. You then have to deliver the sort of performance that will make them want you to keep coming back.

The case study of Touche Ross's (now Deloitte's) Sports Business practice on page 28 is a great example. The firm quickly became a pundit on sports business issues because the media wanted to interview it *because* it had great thought leadership.

6. Visionaries and original thinkers

Many people see thought leadership as about being a visionary – a leader with imagination, insight and boldness.

It is hard to be a genuine visionary, and typically to be taken seriously you need credibility based on past achievement, or at least endorsed by someone famous.

Examples are many and include Steve Jobs (who not only had a vision, but emphatically created it) and James Dyson (ditto).

Billionaire investor Warren Buffett has a simple yet proven investment philosophy that he shares annually at his company's annual general meeting, attracting thousands of devotees to hear his views.

The late Peter Drucker was probably the greatest management theorist. Widely regarded as 'the founder of modern management', he is a great example of someone whose ideas and advice, encapsulated in 39 books translated into 36 languages, were able to bring a legion of followers and exert influence at the highest levels of business and academia.

There are plenty of original thinkers offering informed and thought-provoking commentary, analysis and explanations of business and world events. We'll be looking at how you can achieve the sort of creative thinking that will give you new perspectives on important issues. Perhaps 'original thinkers' are visionaries serving their apprenticeship?

7. The antihero

Not everyone achieves a position of influence for the right reasons. There is a strong and perhaps growing market for antiheroes to share their insights via the media, books, conferences and after-dinner speeches, and films too.

They range from reformed computer hackers to rogue trader Nick Leeson, the man who brought down venerable investment bank Barings. As I write, Jordan Belfort (whose memoirs became the Hollywood hit *The Wolf of Wall Street*), has a speaking tour of America and Britain to cash in further on his notoriety.

While I wouldn't recommend it, the lesson seems to be that if you are going to have a downfall, make it spectacular so you can have a second career writing and speaking about it… and, ideally, selling the film rights too!

8. Celebrity

We are in an age of celebrity, where simply being well known endows people with the credibility to feature in the media, opining on a wide range of subjects outside their areas of expertise.

Even the United Nations is not against taking advantage of this, appointing actors, singers, models and TV presenters as Goodwill Ambassadors and Special Envoys.

This book isn't about turning you into a celebrity (although if you get an invitation to take part in *I'm a Celebrity*, let me know!), but we will be looking at how to take advantage of this fact of modern life to maximise your ability to grab the attention of the media and clients.

9. Adviser to the stars

If you are not famous, borrow some credibility from your famous clients to make yourself more influential too.

The epitome of this was publicist Max Clifford, now residing at HM Prison Littlehey. His reputation for having a long list of celebrity and kiss-&-sell clients made him both wealthy and a regular media commentator, bolstered by his habit of thrusting himself into his clients' spotlights.

More respectable examples range from celebrity hairdresser Nicky Clarke and media lawyer Mark Stephens to Carole Caplin, the 'health and wellbeing consultant' to then Prime Minister Tony Blair's wife Cherie.

Either way, the message is clear and not surprising: the endorsement by, and name-dropping of, famous clients (celebrities, politicians and brands) gives you not just credibility, but some of their valuable halo too.

10. Power brands

Can a brand be a thought leader? No, because it can't have original ideas, these are solely the domain of the people involved in it.

However, strong brands are a huge advantage, and if a brand is well known then those associated with the organisation ride on the added credibility that the brand brings.

If a report carries the name of Harvard Business School, McKinsey or Accenture it will carry more credibility than similar output from Barnsley Business School or a couple of freelance consultants. It will attract more attention and people will probably assume that it benefited from additional rigour and insights.

This may not be fair (there is plenty of weak and self-serving output from big organisations, and lots of great research from smaller firms), but that is one of the advantages of being a large business with a multimillion-pound advertising budget.

What makes a successful thought leader?

People who do thought leadership campaigns are not necessarily the most senior person at their firm. In fact, they may not even be its greatest technical expert (although sometimes they are).

They are not necessarily the people who are the most successful at coming up with a brilliant insight; they are those who are successful in communicating a compelling vision or viewpoint to others in a memorable and persuasive manner.

Many people think technical experts are automatically thought leaders. They aren't. There is a big difference between the two.

A thought leader may well be a technical expert (it is a source of credibility that they have such detailed knowledge about an area) but many technical experts speak in jargon on matters of detail in a manner incomprehensible to anyone who is not another expert.

Brilliant they might be, and almost certainly expensive to hire too. But outside a small group of technical experts they are not understood, carry little influence and are unknown. In fact, for many the depth of their knowledge is a hindrance because they cannot marry it with a breadth of vision.

The people who are successful may be able to talk jargon, but they don't, at least not when communicating with clients, prospects, journalists, and other lay audiences.

Instead they typically have other characteristics. These include:

Purpose

The best thought leaders don't *just* want to win business and make money, although it's usually pretty high on their agenda! They have a purpose: they want to change things, help people and in some specific way make the world a better place.

Their purpose, which maybe they brought with them or maybe it developed as they learnt more about their subject, gives a powerful narrative to their ideas and fuels their energy and passion. It is at the heart of thought leaders and is the key element that marks them out from other experts and colourless spokespeople. They are leaders, not just thinkers.

To be a thought leader – be a *leader* with vision and purpose

Passion

Successful thought leaders aren't dispassionate 'expert witnesses' sifting the facts and coming to logical conclusions like Mr Spock.

They are passionate about the subject – they let it show that they really believe what they are saying and this enthusiasm is infectious for their audiences too. This passion may come from more than intellectual curiosity; it comes from them having developed a desire to change things to help people.

Quite frankly, if you are not passionate it will be hard work becoming and staying knowledgeable on a topic that you find of little interest.

To be a thought leader – find your business mojo!

Knowledge

Great spokespeople have done their homework. This doesn't mean they know everything and it doesn't mean that they don't on occasion say "I don't know about that" – but hopefully not on major areas they should know about!

However, they do have great knowledge about the things you'd expect them to and a lot more on top.

To be a thought leader – know your onions!

Clarity

They can explain their ideas clearly and succinctly in plain English, so that people they are talking to, whether clients, journalists, colleagues or anyone else, can quickly understand their message.

This is the bit many people get wrong, whether experts or juniors; they think that business jargon is needed to impress.

Successful thought leaders may be genetically predisposed to being able to explain things clearly – but I doubt it! It's usually because they have worked hard at getting to the heart of what they want to say and have thought carefully about how to put it across clearly and memorably.

To be a thought leader – capture your idea's essence in simple 'quotable quotes'

Storytellers

They are great at using the other elements that make ideas compelling. They bring in anecdotes, stories and metaphors, together with colourful examples from past and present to create memorable and persuasive explanations.

To be a thought leader – don't just explain, entertain!

Know the detail, but concentrate on the big picture

They are also on top of the detail and data, but they use it very sparingly when communicating – they don't machine-gun listeners with facts. When communicating, their sights stay fixed on the big picture that matters not the small stuff.

To be a thought leader – know the detail, but use data sparingly

Aren't 'know-it-alls'

Thought leadership is all about influencing people, so the best ones don't come across as a patronising know-it-all.

They want to explain and share their ideas, and explore them with the person they are talking to, rather than engage in a debating club-style opportunity to browbeat everyone they come across into submission (although I'm sure they'd be very capable of doing that if they wanted to).

To be a thought leader – aim to win people over, not browbeat them

Contacts and networking

They don't sit in their office all day. They get out and meet lots of people (clients, prospects, referrers, journalists, regulators, influential people, leaders, and other 'go-to people'), discussing and testing their ideas while gaining new insights and contacts.

This also means they know 'the inside' and gossip, not just the 'official version' that gets published, and can call on lots of people to discuss ideas, find out information and generally help 'get things done'. They also know that networking is all about 'give as you get' – ie don't expect favours without giving them too.

To be a thought leader – get out of the office and network

Am I an expert, a bluffer or a thought leader?

Here is a bit of fun to see whether you are on the way to being a thought leader.

Elements of being a thought leader include being knowledgeable *and* recognised for having interesting views and insights.

Complete the following questions and plot your position on the graph to see how you do, but if you do badly, don't throw the book at the wall – it is only an indicator to get you thinking!

Are you well placed to be a thought leader?

Plot your score from Chart 1 on the horizontal axis and your score from Chart 2 on the vertical axis.

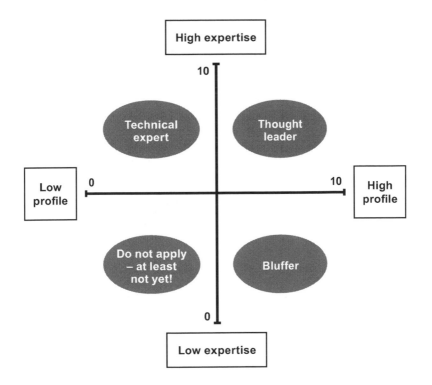

Are you a credible and recognised source of insight?

Fill this in to see how you score	YES	NO
Do you publish research at least once a year?		
Have you received interview or article requests from the media in the past three months?		
Have you been quoted in an article in the national media in the past six months?		
Have you spoken at conferences or other events attended by your clients/prospects in the past six months?		
Have you published a book on your area of expertise?		
Do you have at least 1,000 Twitter followers (or another really powerful social media following)?		
Do prospects often say: "Yes, we have heard of you"?		
Do you get involved in industry lobbying efforts and/or respond to government/regulatory consultations (as a firm, not through an institute)?		
Are you well networked – not only within your industry but also with important influencers like regulators or politicians.		
Do your views or research get re-quoted by others as an authoritative source (whether by competitors, clients, the media etc)?		
SCORE: NUMBER OF YESES		

Are you an expert?

Fill this in to see how you score	YES	NO
Are you an active member of a relevant institute?		
Are you on a working party related to this subject?		
Are you the master of a subject taking years of study?		
Do you speak at events attended by your peers (eg other specialists in this subject)?		
Do you write learned articles for publications read primarily by practitioners in your specialist subject?		
On your business card, do you have at least 10 letters after your name?		
Do clients or colleagues say to you: *"That sounds really complicated... but you're the expert"*?		
Do you love the detail of your area of expertise?		
Have you won awards related to your specialist knowledge?		
Do you get wheeled out to advise clients when they have a difficult problem in your area?		
SCORE: NUMBER OF YESES		

How have you done?

- Thought leader – you are already in a great place. Time to make the most of it. The chapters on 'leveraging the hell' out of your thought leadership will really help.

- Bluffer – you are doing well as a pundit, but you really need to consider if you are building enough authority in this area. The chapters on creating strong insights will really help.

- Technical expert – you are in a great starting position, but you need to make more of your knowledge: it is well known to your colleagues and maybe your competitors, but perhaps not potential clients. This book will help you do this quickly.

- Somewhere around the middle – it's time to build expertise, profile and business by following the steps in this book from Section II onwards.

- Bottom left – you'll want to build your reputation with thought leadership at some point, but basic marketing and knowledge building is required first. Chapter 9's section on Background Research will be particularly helpful as a starting point.

SECTION II
CREATING A SUCCESSFUL THOUGHT LEADERSHIP CAMPAIGN

CHAPTER 4

The vital initial planning for a successful campaign

In the previous chapters we looked at what thought leadership is, why it is important and some of the different ways people have become thought leaders.

Some people have credibility through a track record of success (people such as Sir Richard Branson and Jack Welch) while others gain it through a variety of ways, whether through genuinely ground-breaking ideas (Peter Drucker), the power of celebrity or from having witnessed or taken part in important events.

From now on, we are going to assume you have little of this!

This book is aimed at people in business who need to generate insights and credibility that are thoroughly backed by evidence (whether data, case studies or other corroboration). The sort of thought leadership activity that goes on in a large and growing number of professional, consultancy and business technology firms of all sizes.

In other words, this is the chapter where we start 'doing thought leadership' and no more setting the scene about what it is!

Over the next few chapters we will take you through, in practical steps, everything you need to do to produce a successful thought leadership programme.

This will involve explaining and applying the methodology successfully applied at numerous businesses by Kelso Consulting, my business. Some clients have been large, but many have been SMEs with limited resources.

The remaining part of the book is very much like a recipe in that respect: follow the steps and you will have something successful at the end!

The stages to Kelso Consulting's sure-fire thought leadership methodology are:

1. Identify *your* business challenge.

2. Identify the area of focus for your campaign.

3. Create the business case and political buy-in.

4. Background research and knowledge building.

5. Create your hypothesis.

6. Substantiate your hypothesis, its impact and the consequences of your breakthrough insights.

7. Create attention-grabbing content.

8. A strong and ongoing marketing and sales campaign to generate leads and create clients.

9. Review, refine, repeat.

The first thing you may notice about it is that all the fun stuff (like the brainstorming ideas to create the breakthrough insight, and using the output to generate lots of new clients) is only a small part of the overall activity. It also comes relatively late down the path.

Delivering successful thought leadership: Kelso Consulting's methodology

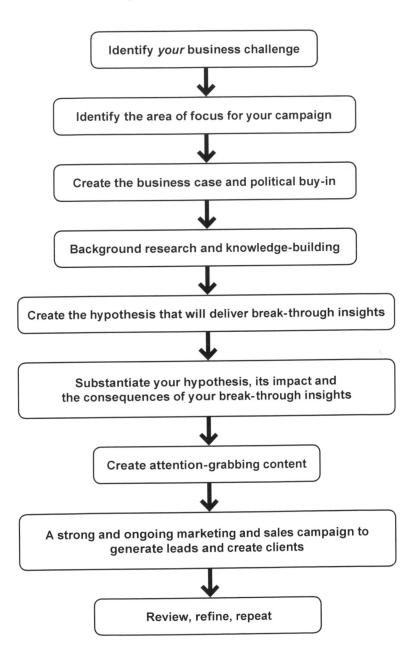

Identify *your* business challenge

Identify the area of focus for your campaign

Create the business case and political buy-in

Background research and knowledge-building

Create the hypothesis that will deliver break-through insights

Substantiate your hypothesis, its impact and the consequences of your break-through insights

Create attention-grabbing content

A strong and ongoing marketing and sales campaign to generate leads and create clients

Review, refine, repeat

Most of the steps are the perhaps dull-sounding planning and preparation – the sort of stuff people often like to skip, especially the first time around.

Let me be clear: when I see thought leadership campaigns go wrong, often the root cause is inadequate preparation. The effect of this is:

- After much effort they feel they have picked the wrong area; and/or

- Momentum runs out, whether through inadequate senior buy-in or it simply going nowhere; and/or

- The findings produced are weak and do not have impact; or

- The findings are great and the report wonderful, but little is done with it, because they've failed to plan for the most important part: promoting it strongly.

Having the brainstorms, issuing press releases and doing interviews are great fun. They are also very important.

However, my experience is that many people overemphasise these elements and in their race to get to them, jeopardise the project through inadequate planning and preparation, only to rue it later.

The approach in this book is all about delivering a great result every time, or at least as frequently as is humanly possible, and for this you need to remember the six Ps: ***Proper Planning Prevents Piss Poor Performance.***

Identifying your business challenge

The starting point, and the key to ensuring you get off to the best possible start, is to work hard at identifying why it is really important for *your* business to invest a lot of time and resources in a thought leadership project.

Benefits of a thought leadership position:

The benefits of being well recognised as an expert include:

- Differentiation
- You are easy for others to recommend
- Premium pricing (ie reassuringly expensive)
- Providing added value
- Outcompete large competitors
- Safe choice in an uncertain world

In addition, it allows you to move from selling on price and features to consultative and challenger selling. Benefits from this include:

- Move from supplier relationship to peer-to-peer relationship
- Earlier involvement in procurement process (or avoiding it altogether)

This also allows you to overcome the senior sales challenge: 'Senior people do not want to be sold to until they are in buying mode... but when they go into buying mode, they have typically already made up their mind as to who they want to use.'

It might seem so obvious to you that 'it goes without saying' and you want to rush past this step.

Don't!

If you are going to spend a lot of time and resources on an initiative, you need to be clear it is going to solve a major problem or create a sizeable opportunity. The clearer your thinking is at this stage, the easier your life will be as the project continues – both for getting buy-in from colleagues and also in terms of making sure the project delivers what you really need.

A – Start at the top, with your business's vision, mission and strategy

Most businesses have visions, missions and values. Many are bland or vague, generate cynicism and quickly get forgotten.

At other firms they are really important and guide strategy, plans and objectives.

Whichever category your firm falls into, benefits come from doing things properly. You need to know how solving your problem (presumably with a thought leadership programme) fits into delivering the strategy and vision.

So what I'd like you to do is fill in the chart below. If you would rather not write in the book, this chart and all the others can be downloaded from www.kelsopr.com/thought-leadership-manual-resources

It is really important that you do – ultimately your thought leadership and marketing need to be clearly linked to delivering your business's strategy and vision.

If you don't have a vision and mission, fill in what you can, but you are not in a great position and you need to sort it out. If your vision is simply 'to grow' or something similar, then that really is a D-minus (must try harder!). It needs to be SMART (specific, measurable, achievable, realistic and with a timescale), like JFK's vision in the chart on the following page.

If you don't have a strategy, stop and get one! Creating a mission, vision, strategy and plan for your practice is beyond the scope of this book; these are huge areas with countless books already.

However, there is a strong assumption in this book that you have these elements in place – and if you don't, I'm emphatically advising you to get them in place. After all, if you don't know what you are looking to achieve, how will you know if a lot of time invested in thought leadership will get you there?

The sorts of problems thought leadership can solve:

- The important people don't know our name
- We don't have credibility with decision makers
- We don't get on to the tender lists
- We get on to the tenders but don't have the right relationships
- We don't know enough to use a 'challenge a sale' approach
- There's a big problem/opportunity facing our clients we need to alert them to
- We are being commoditised or otherwise moving down the value chain
- Great expertise but no one knows about it

Mission, vision and strategy

Add your practice's details below	Write your mission, vision and strategy statements here	What they are...
The mission statement of my firm (or practice area) is...		A mission statement is a summary of your business's reason for existing – your market, your service and why the client should choose you.
The vision of my firm (or practice area) is...		A vision statement sets out the desired future state – what you want to achieve. It provides inspiration and focus.
Our strategy for achieving our vision is...		The broad approach you will take that will move you from your current position to the desired position (ie achieving your vision).
EXAMPLE		*US President John F Kennedy delivered one of the best vision statements of all time on 25 May 1961 in a landmark speech to a joint session of Congress. Here is how it might look...*
The mission statement		Restore American pride and demonstrate the pre-eminence of the USA over communism by regaining the initiative from the USSR in the Space Race.
The vision		"I believe that this nation should commit itself to achieving the goal, before this decade is out, of landing a man on the Moon and returning him safely to Earth."
Nasa's strategy for achieving the vision		Build and launch a series of rockets, each going farther than the previous, until Nasa gains the technology, experience and know-how to deliver the vision – which it did on 21 July 1969.

Our strategy is 'to target everyone'

I am not going to opine about what makes a good strategy, but I will about weak ones, as they will cause problems!

I do come across a lot of businesses, especially partnerships and consultancies, whose strategy is something along the lines of 'we target all businesses', 'we target all SMEs' or 'we target all large businesses'.

Now, there is a big difference between who you are prepared to work for, if they knocked on your door unprompted, and those who you actively target as clients because you are particularly well placed to offer them distinctive and valuable services.

If your strategy is along the lines of those caricatured above (ie 'we target everybody'), then it is not a strategy! Targeting everybody, or nearly everybody, is not a strategy, it is an absence of strategy.

This sort of woolly thinking will almost certainly lead to bland research and poor results down the line.

If you are in this position, in the first instance it is not a thought leadership problem, it is simply a 'thought' problem!

Before continuing with thought leadership, you absolutely need to be clear about where you are in the market, your points of differentiation and your value proposition. Given these, which are the segments you are particularly targeting?

B – What is the opportunity, problem or challenge you really want to tackle?

Having looked at the big goals for your firm or practice (mission, vision, strategy) it is time to consider the challenge that solving is so important that you want to invest time and money in a thought leadership initiative to tackle it.

What exactly is the opportunity, problem or other dilemma that you face and need to overcome with a thought leadership initiative?

Once you have thought about it, write it in the first row of the chart on page 70.

When filling it out, make sure you don't put something vague like 'no one has heard of us' or 'we don't have enough sales leads'. These might be good starting points, but delve a bit deeper to the specific problem.

For instance, if you are tempted to say 'no one has heard of us', consider exactly why it is a problem. Presumably you want work from certain types of people and businesses and there is a reason they haven't heard of you, and what is the negative outcome of this?

Here is how 'no one has heard of us' might instead be more specifically put for an example firm: "*We are an American technology business that is new to London. While we are well known in the US market, we are not getting invited to tenders here. The relevant decision makers and specifiers at our targets (chief information officers and procurement teams at the 15 largest UK and European general insurers), seem unaware of our brand and the solution we provide.*"

If you have not done so already, do spend time discussing this challenge with colleagues to get beyond the symptoms and generalities to specifics of the real underlying problem. If it changes, you can write in the improved version as we go along!

Having clearly identified the challenge you are tackling, it is time to set out the evidence for it and the implications of ignoring it in the chart below.

Citing evidence

This part is also really important. Citing evidence (preferably backed with some numbers and even market data) helps clarify your thinking. It is also going to be needed later when you want to get buy-in from colleagues.

What is the implication of doing nothing?

Often in budgeting people consider carefully the cost of doing something to tackle a problem, but not the cost of failing to do anything. Don't fall into that trap: on row three, add in the implications of not tackling the opportunity or challenge you have identified.

Not only will this help you convince yourself whether it is a problem worth solving, these details will be vital for later on when you have to get buy-in from colleagues and budget holders.

C – What are the obstacles you must overcome?

Once you have finished the first section in the chart below, work on through the other two parts: what the future will look like with the problem solved, and what are the obstacles you need to overcome to achieve it.

Not only will setting out the future help motivate you to achieve it, but it is going to be essential for you and your colleagues to keep your eyes on achieving this as the project continues.

It is also very useful for the next steps, which involve defining the specific problems or opportunities you are tackling and other elements of the thought leadership project as you proceed. After all, a thought leadership project needs to tackle some of the big things you have identified in the chart below that are stopping you achieving the success you seek.

To download this and other charts in the book, please go to www.kelsopr.com/thought-leadership-manual-resources

The challenges and obstacles that face your business

1. Identifying and setting out your challenge clearly

Our specific problem/ challenge/opportunity is...	
Evidence for it includes...	
Implications of ignoring it or doing nothing are?	

2. What does the future look like with the challenge resolved?

If we solved this problem/ met the challenge, our new position would be...	
Evidence that solving this problem (or seizing this opportunity) is realistic...	
What will we then be able to do that we can't currently do...	

3. What are the major obstacles that you must overcome and the milestones that you must achieve?

What is stopping you being in this successful position?	
What steps are needed to solve this problem or exploit this opportunity?	

CHAPTER 5

Creating the buy-in for thought leadership

In the previous chapter you identified important challenges (whether opportunities or problems) you must tackle in order to deliver your practice's strategy successfully.

You've identified particular challenges you want to solve with a thought leadership campaign and have written it loud and proud on the chart in the previous chapter.

At this point it's tempting to charge into the office of your boss and announce: "We have problem X and I want to solve it by embarking on a thought leadership programme by doing research and announcing some wonderful findings to the world. Give me lots of money so I can get on with it straight away!"

You'll be the best judge of how to get things approved in your organisation, and maybe that is how things get done… but probably not.

There will be people whose approval you need when it comes to money. No doubt, you'll need to generate some sort of consensus that this is the right way for you and the firm to spend lots of resources.

It is also important to take into account your firm's existing reputation. Some colleagues will see 'something different' as a risk or a challenge to maintaining that which they regard as existing value.

In fact, you will need to take your colleagues through four stages progressively. They are:

1. If it does not exist already, a consensus needs to be built that this is an important problem that needs to be solved (this may well have already been highlighted from your business planning process).

2. Again, if it is not present already, a consensus needs to be created that a thought leadership project is part of the right approach.

3. Where agreement on the need and approach exists, you will then need agreement on the broad theme or area the campaign will cover.

4. When all of the above is agreed, you will need agreement on the specific form it will take and the budget. Here you are on the home straight, but still with hurdles. Getting agreement for the specifics of what the project will actually involve and how much money and other resources are available can be the biggest battles.

Each area can prove tricky, depending on the firm. For instance, where a firm has done little thought leadership previously, particular problem stages could be building a consensus for trying a thought leadership project and its cost (stages 2 and 4).

By contrast, at firms with a track record of such projects, these areas might not be particularly controversial, but the theme may lead to a lot of controversy.

For Steve Blundell, a leading adviser to larger professional firms and a director with strategy advisers Redstone Consultants, it is stage 3 that is typically the most problematic with his clients.

He says: "The particular challenge for big firms is getting an idea that on the one hand is sufficiently broad-based to be politically and commercially viable, but not so broad as to be banal. Sometimes it can be a struggle to balance these.

"Assuming that you get the idea, you still have to negotiate common problems, such as the idea being too technical (so not of interest to the reader) or not aligned with the firm's strategy, in which case partners will be unlikely to use it."

Later in the book we will be tackling these problems highlighted by Steve, while in this section our focus is getting you to stage 2: getting a consensus around the problem and the need for some sort of thought leadership project to tackle it.

You'll no doubt have plenty of experience of attempting to persuade your colleagues to your viewpoint, and hopefully know how to do it well.

It can prove particularly difficult in organisations new to this sort of initiative, where problems might come through resistance to the idea but may also take the form of unrealistic expectations about speed and likely impact.

In such situations consider creating smaller, easy-to-deploy initiatives that can be 'door openers' for larger initiatives once they have proved their value.

It is particularly worth noting that your first thought leadership initiative will be the hardest; you are learning on the job and creating some of the infrastructure as you go. So the more limited the objective, the easier it will be to achieve and the less likely you are to hit problems of overrunning or under-delivering.

All the ins and outs of persuading doubters are beyond the scope of this book. However, one element that I'd highlight is the importance of thinking strategically. For each stage, map out the people involved, their agenda, what they have bought into and what will motivate them.

One approach is to classify people by four types of role they will play in the decisions:

1. Budget: the key person, the one who gives budgetary approval.

2. Supporter: influential people who agree with you.

3. Blocker: influential people with the ability to stop it happening.

4. Irrelevant: anyone who is not one of the other types.

There are lots of systems for classifying people (do use one of these if you prefer), but the main point is to think strategically about whose support you need and how you are going to get it, while preventing someone opposed to it from blocking or otherwise derailing your efforts.

Getting buy-in for thought leadership – mapping the decision makers

Use the chart below to plan your charm offensive and record progress. But don't write about your colleagues in this book in case they read it! Instead download it from www.kelsopr.com/thought-leadership-manual-resources… and keep it at home just in case!

With the work that has been done in the earlier chapters (not to mention the list of objections you may face, many of which are covered in Chapter 6), you are well placed and have the content to use to present a strong case to your colleagues to get them to stage 2.

Stage 3 is where things start going from theory to practice: what you are actually looking to find out and achieve.

This is really important as weak work here can lead to the project going in the wrong direction or producing feeble findings. The next chapter tackles it in detail.

Map the decision-makers to have a clear plan for winning their support

Person	Role	Which stages have they bought into?	Their agenda	Next step	Buttons to push

FOR EXAMPLE:

Person	Role	Which stages have they bought into?	Their agenda	Next step	Buttons to push
Managing Partner	Budget	First stage (agree with you on the key problem to be solved)	Control budget and achieve growth	Gain buy-in for a TL approach (move him to become a supporter)	His need to deliver the firm's strategy and growth target, as well as delivering budget and billable hour targets
Marketing Director	Blocker	None	Doesn't like anything 'not created here' by his team	Attempt to bring onside by making him feel involved. Try to convert him into a supporter	His team will be closely involved
Head of Corporate Finance	Supporter	Three	You have privately agreed to cover a theme that will also benefit her team	Get her to speak up when this is discussed at management meetings	Keep her onside by highlighting the relevance to her team
Practice Manager	Irrelevant	Don't bother – concentrate on those who matter on this issue			

CHAPTER 6

Overcoming problems and prevarications

The best way to be unsuccessful is not to attempt something important in the first place.

In this section I tackle some of the prevarications I hear people say that cause them to defer and avoid thought leadership programmes.

Maybe some are in your head, or maybe you will hear them from your colleagues. You will have read some of the case studies in this book of hugely successful thought leadership campaigns; all of these had their objectors who needed to be overcome.

I don't know enough/other people know more than me

The first point is that no one knows everything, no matter how much they think they do.

Of course, if you and your firm want to compete with such knowledgeable competitors you need to do something about it!

It is relatively straightforward to develop a niche area and become an expert on this, and then broaden out as you gain experience and knowledge. The methodology in this book will help you do this: start small and build up.

I do not have enough time

We are all busy people: work, family, hobbies, other commitments.

Everyone only has finite time in the day, so time spent on this has to be carved out somewhere.

Is it simply a question of: 'Is it a priority and are you willing to do it?'

Ultimately, even the busiest people can find time to do something if they want to.

In this book we'll be looking at how to set clear purposes, goals, a realistic timetable and ways of both minimising your effort and maximising your 'bang for the buck'.

Don't think that thought leadership must involve hundreds of hours; set goals to the time you have available, and build it into your existing routine.

For instance, if you have four hours a week available, you are not going to be able to 'knock McKinsey off their perch'. But that is around 200 hours over a year and, used well, think what you can achieve with this. You can certainly find time to talk to clients and contacts, ask them about their biggest challenges, brainstorm with your colleagues and write an article or blog every few weeks or a white paper every quarter.

We're too busy with fee-earning work

If your firm is perpetually flat out with high-quality, lucrative projects for great clients, you are indeed in a fortunate position and long may it continue.

However, sometimes busyness is not so good and it's worth scratching beneath the surface.

For instance, is busyness caused by lots of small value projects when what you really need is better clients who will give you chunkier and more lucrative work? So, in other words, you are busy but not terribly profitable.

Is the busyness due to poor leverage with senior and experienced people doing the work that should be done by more junior people?

Is the busyness because you have to do a lot of pitches as the result of a poor win ratio? A good win rate for proposals is not one in four or one in five; a good win rate is 75% or above, since you should be weeding out ones where you have limited chance in order to concentrate your time and effort on winning the likely ones.

Is your busyness through you having to provide, year after year, the same services for a lower margin against increased competition?

It is worth reflecting on whether it is 'good' busyness or 'bad' busyness. If the latter, it is time to stop chasing your tail. Maybe a strategy utilising a thought leadership approach is exactly what is needed to break out of the cycle?

I might say something that isn't correct

This worry is clearly the very embodiment of inner self-doubt leaping out and taking control of your tongue!

It's good to have a small measure of self-doubt as that pushes you to prepare harder (after all, over-confidence can be a big enemy).

You are a qualified, educated person who deals with clients all the time; you are most unlikely to allow yourself to say something stupid.

On top of that, if you follow the process in this book, not to mention the sort of background research and preparation you would do anyway as a competent professional, you can be pretty sure that what you are saying is sensible.

In several places we highlight the importance of peer reviewing your thought leadership; this is perhaps the biggest and most effective safeguard that what you say will be really interesting.

In fact, it is not being wrong you have to worry about, it is being bland!

However, on occasions it does happen. People get things wrong.

While I wouldn't recommend making a habit of it, people get over making mistakes, move on and continue to have successful careers and impressive reputations.

The world is full of experts who've got it wrong on occasions. Sometimes it is a small error, and sometimes it is big. Here are some examples from which you can take heart that the odd 'cock-up' is not going to hurt your firm:

- For instance, there is no shortage of economists and other banking experts who completely failed to see the financial crisis coming (indeed, many didn't recognise it when it was upon us). Most were then wrong about the length of the crisis, and they also failed to see the recovery when it started to happen.

- One of the most famous and lauded business books, *In Search of Excellence*, was co-written by uber guru Tom Peters. It highlights various companies as role models, but after it was published, many quickly became very 'un-excellent'. This didn't hold back his career or earning capacity, perhaps even the reverse.

- A couple of examples from Touche Ross (now Deloitte) from my time there:

  ○ On page 28 you will see the case study of one of the accountancy profession's most successful thought leadership initiatives: its football accounts research. The first report contained a controversial statement, and a highly litigious club chairman threatened to sue. This didn't derail the project, in this case it had quite the reverse effect.

○ When I was working in its press office, I issued a press release (in those days by post) from one of its top tax experts. A day or so later, I was called by *The Sunday Times* querying one of the examples. There was indeed an error in the calculations.

After a short deliberation we issued a corrected version and asked journalists to ignore the earlier version. It was the end of the matter and no journalist ever mentioned it, and the tax specialist continued to be a highly popular and trusted spokesperson with the media.

In politics ministers have their careers ruined not by their initial mistakes, but by subsequent attempts to cover it up. So with mistakes, it is not a mistake that is the defining moment, but how you deal with it.

People might disagree with us

Honestly, people do say this to me! It is pretty inevitable. If some people don't disagree with your views then they must be uncontentious, bland and mainstream.

If you aren't prepared for this, you really aren't ready for a leadership role. The whole point of new insights is that many people will disagree with them, at least at first.

If our insights are so great, shouldn't we keep them to ourselves?

It's a perfectly legitimate question and sometimes the answer is yes.

You should think carefully about whom you share your intellectual capital with and in what way.

There are some elements you may want to restrict to clients. There may be some parts that will give you a great advantage and you don't want to share at all. There will be other elements you want to share widely.

The decision is yours, and it should be a conscious and deliberate one.

What I would ask you to think about is whether you are in such a unique position that you are going to have insights rival firms aren't capable of if they make the effort.

Problems can befall even the best of us

McKinsey, probably the world's top strategy consultancy, marked the 50th anniversary of its *McKinsey Quarterly* with an article attempting to look 50 years into the future.

Financial Times columnist Lucy Kellaway took issue and described it as a "sorry exercise in windy platitudes… as for originality, if the best McKinsey can do after years of study is say that technology, globalisation and ageing will feature in the next 50 years, a robot could have come up with that in a jiffy."

No doubt when the article appeared it was not the best day the McKinsey authors had ever had, and maybe their press officer decided to lie low too.

But McKinsey and the authors continue undiminished. Hopefully they took the same attitude as when the same happened to Accenture a few years before. That time one of its directors was pilloried in her column for writing a letter full of management gobbledegook.

He laughed it off as a backhanded compliment. If you are important enough to be criticised in one of the most read columns in the world's top business newspaper, he stoically but rightly reasoned, then you know you are well above all the people who don't merit any attention.

The biggest danger I find is not that someone will pinch your ideas. The biggest danger facing thought leadership campaigns is that you will sit on them too long and someone else will steal your thunder, relegating you from innovative thinker to 'me-too'.

You may have discussions with colleagues who prevail upon you to keep all of your findings back to prevent competitors being informed by your hard work. If so, be specific about exactly which finding it is that is so distinctive and cannot be shared. Do you really think other people won't come to this conclusion in the near future?

Steve Blundell of Redstone Consultants recounts one such experience: "I was working with a large international law firm that started a thought leadership project in 2011 with a timetable to complete in four months. There was a lot of interest from its clients and contacts we interviewed on the subject, and a real desire to hear what the firm had to say.

"But after 18 months the firm was still caught up in internal wrangles about how to service the work that would be generated by the initiative. One month before the much-delayed launch, a major consulting firm published a report which stole about three-quarters of their thunder!

"Sadly the delays meant that so much of the impact was lost, they ended up looking much less thought leaders than thought followers! It also underlines the fact that your thought leadership initiatives don't just face competition from your rivals, you are also competing with businesses from other sectors too."

We aren't credible enough in this market

That is a big problem and you need to overcome it. Thought leadership offers a powerful way of quickly becoming better known and respected, as long as you have some great expertise you can build on.

We don't have anything interesting to say

Ditto! That is a big problem and you need to overcome it. Thought leadership offers a powerful way of quickly becoming well informed and creating something interesting to say. The next section will show you exactly how to do this.

CHAPTER 7

Getting ready to 'leverage the hell' out of your thought leadership

"We need to concentrate on leveraging the hell out of it," was a great phrase a CEO client of mine used vividly to his team to highlight his desire for them to make the very most of the thought leadership report that had just been finished.

The marketing team had decided to 'wait and see' what promotional activity should be done until after the impending press launch had happened. The new and impressive reports were consequently sitting around the office, unused, in the boxes from the printer.

It was a strong and needed intervention from the CEO. He could see that having spent valuable resources on the report it was about to die through over-caution and inaction.

His intervention turned around the situation.

Don't get yourself in this position!

To get every drop of value from your thought leadership efforts, you need to be planning from the outset what you are going to do with it, not waiting until the end.

The important elements you need to be thinking about early so that you too can 'leverage the hell' out of your thought leadership activity are your:

- Audiences – who are you trying to reach?
- Content – what will you provide them with? eg white paper, presentation, book, etc
- Channels – the best ways to reach your audiences, eg press coverage, website, direct mail, adverts
- Plan for ensuring your thought leadership ideas reach the right people in the right way

Once you've developed your breakthrough insights you will want to get working as quickly as possible on reports, white papers and the other content your campaign will need. And once these are ready you will want to utilise them as quickly as possible while they are fresh.

You certainly don't want to be sitting around for weeks while plans are drawn and mailing lists sourced.

Instead, get the basics sorted even before the research begins. What content are you going to want at the end of it, and is the 'marketing infrastructure' in place for a successful campaign, or does it need sorting out?

What content will you need?

First of all, you need to think carefully about your target audiences: the key people you want to reach, such as clients, prospects, referrers or other influencers.

The more specific you are about these, and the more you can 'get to know them', the better (for instance: their characteristics, likes and preferences as a broad group), as you will want to deliver your thought leadership to them in the way that has the maximum impact.

To give a stark example: if you have prospects who are visual and techie types with short attention spans then a long text document is wrong. A podcast is not so good for them, but great for people who drive or travel a lot.

Academics, actuaries and engineers tend to like arguments backed up with lots of detail and evidence, and they will invest the time digesting it. A one-page summary and a pretty infographic alone aren't going to work for them, but this would work well, perhaps, for getting the attention of heads of creative agencies.

It is also tempting to think mainly about all the countless businesses you don't know, that you want to end up as your clients, and to focus your attention on them. But it is those closest to you that are most likely to buy and recommend you, so the important targets to think about particularly are:

- Your fellow partners and/or sales team (for cross-selling to existing clients and prospects)
- Existing clients
- Your referrers and potential referrers
- Your firm's alumni
- Alliance partners
- Important opinion formers and associations/institutes you belong to

Different types of content are considered more fully in Chapter 15.

In the meantime, you should map out all your main targets and start to consider what content you will need for communicating with them.

Identify the best way to communicate with your targets

Target audiences	Are they detail or 'big ideas' people	In the office or 'on the move'?	Left brain or right brain?	Where do they get their information?	What are the right channels to reach them?

FOR EXAMPLE:

Target audiences	Are they detail or 'big ideas' people	In the office or 'on the move'?	Left brain or right brain?	Where do they get their information?	What are the right channels to reach them?
Heads of London-based creative agencies	Big ideas and visual	Mobile and PC mainly (and face-to-face)	Right brain creatives – like things that are new and eye-catching	Creative sector trade press; Networking and gossiping; National quality papers; *Evening Standard*; *Channel 4 News*; Radio 4 and 5; Twitter (and Google)	Trade press; Business lunch; Breakfast seminar; Social media; Email; PR
Our colleagues in the corporate finance department	Big ideas and 'pound signs'	PC and mobile, but many like paper; Big networkers	Left brain – analytical	*Financial Times* and eFinancialnews; CF trade titles; News alerts; Radio 5; Gossip with colleagues; Social media (and Google)	Evening presentation (with booze); Individual face-to-face follow-up; Walk their corridor regularly

Getting your marketing infrastructure ready

When you come to launch your big findings to the world, the last thing you want is to find that your marketing lists are two years out of date and the access code to the corporate Twitter account was lost last year.

The earlier you assess what marketing infrastructure you need, the better, so you can find out its condition and what is needed to ensure it is ready for your campaign.

Where it needs fixing or bolstering, you need to decide whether the benefits are worth the effort and, indeed, if you have the time and resources to achieve this.

The following table is a good starting point to begin the process with your team.

What 'Marketing Infrastructure' do you have in place (and what do you need to sort out)?

Marketing and infrastructure element	How would you grade its current status?				What are we going to do? (No action, investigate, experiment, fix, bolster*)	Who is sorting this out and by when?
	WE'VE NOT DONE THIS BEFORE	POOR / OBSOLETE CONDITION	CAN BE BROUGHT UP TO PAR	GOOD CONDITION		
DIRECT MARKETING						
Email/postal mailing lists A suitable list of clients, prospects and/or referrals – including name, company, job title, email, postal address and telephone number						
List of named prospects and targets, ranked by priority						
Phone skills The ability to 'pick up the phone' to prospects and make it happen						
ONLINE						
Website with good functionality and ability to capture visitors' email						
'Search engine optimise' your web pages						
Social media: LinkedIn, Facebook, Google+, Twitter, etc						
GoogleAd programme						

* **Experiment** = We will use this project as an opportunity to learn with this channel.   **Fix** = has problems that we will sort out so it can be used.   **Bolster** = This is in good shape but we want to build it further.

90

What 'Marketing Infrastructure' do you have in place (and what do you need to sort out)? CONTINUED

Marketing and infrastructure element	How would you grade its current status?				What are we going to do? (No action, investigate, experiment, fix, bolster*)	Who is sorting this out and by when?
	WE'VE NOT DONE THIS BEFORE	POOR / OBSOLETE CONDITION	CAN BE BROUGHT UP TO PAR	GOOD CONDITION		
OTHER PROMOTIONAL ACTIVITY						
An established **PR programme** and/or strong press know-how						
Advertising experience						
Industry events: sponsorship, speaking and exhibiting						
A programme of events: seminars, webinars, etc, organised by our firm						
Other elements that are important to your business or market, eg events, directories, conferences, etc						

* **Experiment** = We will use this project as an opportunity to learn with this channel. **Fix** = has problems that we will sort out so it can be used. **Bolster** = This is in good shape but we want to build it further.

Getting your 'launch' plan ready

For most readers of this book, the very best way for you to maximise the value of your impending thought leadership will be to get your ideas out fast and hard, exploiting their novelty as much as you possibly can while they are fresh, relevant and original.

You need a plan that delivers a great launch, but it shouldn't stop there; you want a plan that enables you to continue exploiting it for many months.

When people think of marketing, they tend to think of things like brochures, websites, events, case studies, golf days, press releases – the sorts of thing that the marketing department typically does. In fact, successful marketing is all about strategy, regularity, consistency of message, building a relationship of trust, and focusing on the people most likely to buy your services.

You want your campaign to deliver this – not just a one-off splurge, but the building and strengthening of relationships through activity that lasts weeks and months, not just a few days.

For instance, if you think about the buying process in most firms, it is unlikely that one emailed white paper is going to make an executive suddenly ditch a supplier and use you instead.

Resist the urge to launch everything at once, as if it were a Hollywood blockbuster, then breathe a huge sigh of relief and pretty much leave it alone. Instead of having a 'launch' campaign that lasts a few weeks, have a plan that utilises your work over many months or longer.

Your plan needs to communicate in a sustained manner so you build sufficient recognition and credibility that your prospects will consider you a trustworthy supplier.

I suggest you treat your thought leadership as though you were providing a great meal of several courses at a top restaurant: each course should be outstanding, but also make your prospects eagerly await the next one.

The campaign should help you deliver the necessary consistency and regularity that builds up a relationship of trust and positions you as the natural choice for when they are in buying mode, rather than trying to cajole them into buying with a sudden one-off burst of activity at the launch that is not followed up.

CHAPTER 8

Measuring the impact

Many business-to-business firms are excellent at measuring the effectiveness of their marketing, sales and promotional activity.

They analyse all sorts of aspects of the traffic to their website, tweaking and experimenting with it to get the absolute optimal impact with visitors. They study the open rates and click-throughs of their emails to know the optimum time, content and headline to use. Inbound leads are tracked so that they know their source and profitability; maybe they even profile them for further targeted activity.

They use the wealth of data that's available and they analyse it to keep track of how the business is doing and what's working and what isn't. They also know the ROI for particular projects, like thought leadership campaigns.

By contrast, many businesses (particularly many professional firms) are woeful in this area and only track chargeable time and billings.

These are vital measures for how the business is currently doing, but are poor for helping understand important questions, such as: "Was this campaign a good investment of our time?"

It needn't be like this. Many firms have huge amounts of data that they aren't aware of – website visitor data, for instance. If they use an emailing system there is lots of information here, while their time sheet system and CRM can (and probably do) capture all sorts of useful insights.

Making use of this information is going to be vital if you are to answer important questions such as:

- How much time and money was spent on the project, and how was this against budget?

- What sales were generated – to both new and existing clients?

- How much fee income has been generated by the project?

- What activity was undertaken around the firm to utilise the report?

- What was the project's return on investment and is it worth doing again?

To answer these questions, you need to decide what you are going to measure at the early stages so that you can have appropriate tracking and targets in place.

For instance, if you want to track time spent on it (a very useful thing) you'll need to set up a charge code or some way of tracking on your time sheet. The same goes for having a way to identify leads and track them through their conversion as customers so you can identify income generated.

At some firms the infrastructure will be in place and it can happen relatively simply. At others, you will have to improvise and think how best to utilise what is available.

Either way, it is your responsibility as the person either leading or managing the project to ensure that the normal management discipline of target setting, data collection, analysis and review continues throughout the project.

The important point is to include this in your planning stage.

Input, output or outcome measures

With thought leadership, we are all in the business of changing attitudes in order to influence behaviour. Often, you'll want to influence people by making them more likely to get in touch with your business. With established clients you'll want to make them more likely to buy more.

We can distinguish between three sorts of measures: input, output and outcome:

- Input measures are typically the time and resources you spend on it.

- Output measures will be what you do with it – number of white papers, press releases, seminars, etc.

- Outcome measures will be the indicators of changed behaviour – such as inquiries from prospects, traffic to your website, new projects and other indicators that things have changed as a result of the campaign.

The inputs and outputs are typically the easiest to measure and are important for ensuring it is on track, but it is the outcomes that assess the project's success or failure. Ultimately, you want to be able to say to your boss and colleagues: "The thought leadership project I led generated 10 new clients for the firm, has helped generate £150k of fees and has doubled the number of leads we get through the website – a 500% return on investment already."

Make sure you are able to do this by having the metrics in place. Some thoughts are in the boxed item on page 99, but don't use too many – just a few!

Example – Accenture's ROI measures

Terry Corby, whose roles have included being in charge of Accenture's thought leadership globally, highlights how measuring to ensure projects deliver a strong return on investment is really important to the firm.

He says: "Accenture has a large central thought leadership team working on a small number of big themes that are important to the firm, such as the impact of us moving to a 'multi-polar world', while individual practices also can have their own programmes utilising this, or on specific themes relevant to their markets.

"It used various measurements to gauge the success of these initiatives. But you don't have to be an enormous firm like Accenture to be on top of the metrics. The sorts of areas we measured to assess if the return on investment had been good included: the impact with clients, such as the number of new leads, discussions and proposals; publicity generated; work won; and other engagement with key audiences.

"We particularly measure the internal take up of the report. For firms of any size, getting your colleagues to utilise the material with their clients and contacts is key – this was the most important area for assessing if an initiative was successful."

Measuring output or outcome?

It is straightforward to measure inputs (time and money) and also outputs (press releases, reports, Tweets, etc).

The key to assessing if the campaign was a success is to define and measure outcomes: what did you want to change and did it happen?

Example measures include:

Inputs:

- Time
- Money

Outputs:

- Reports produced
- Press releases issued
- Webpages created
- Blogs posted
- Case studies written
- Social media messages (eg number of Tweets, etc) sent
- Direct marketing emails sent

Outcome measures:

- Traffic to your website, particularly traffic to particular landing pages; arrivals using key words relevant to the subject; downloads of the report
- Comments made by others on social media
- Securing a prominent position on Google (for a search phrase related to the project)
- Requests for meetings and actual meetings with prospects
- Invitations to tender received
- Requests for proposals
- Press coverage generated
- Meetings with clients
- Meetings at clients with people it's been difficult to reach previously
- Meetings with referrers
- Sales related to the subject of your campaign

Case study – How will you know if you succeed?

With one of my accountancy clients it was clear in an emphatic way that their campaign was working.

They had started the campaign because they were in the position of being a 'best kept secret' in their specialist market. Their insurance sector clients thought they were great and valued the huge levels of technical expertise the partners had – yet no one outside their client base knew about them and they were never invited for audit tenders.

With a major regulatory change happening that would affect all firms in the sector, they launched a campaign to highlight their expertise, increase brand awareness and build contacts with finance directors and other decision makers.

A thought leadership programme of bimonthly 'countdown' guides containing authoritative management advice for preparing for the changes, combined with press coverage and briefing seminars, brought a strong reaction.

Seminar attendees were called by a telesales agency to arrange meetings with the firm's partners.

Over a relatively short period of time, the result was profound. Within a year of the campaign being devised the firm went from 'never on the tender list' to 'always on the tender list' within their niche market and they had won their biggest ever audit.

It is important that you have targets in place so you know when your campaign is succeeding – or, if it is not, so action can be taken to get back on track. Through the way it was devised there were lots of clear indicators of success that could be measured. These included:

- Requests for newsletters
- Feedback from clients
- Attendance at seminars
- Number of follow-up meetings following the seminars
- Increase in number of audit tender invitations

SECTION III CREATING BREAKTHROUGH IDEAS

Selecting the theme for your thought leadership

The previous section of the book included building up consensus at your business regarding the need for thought leadership as well as initial preparation you need to consider.

This section is all about creating the great insights and breakthrough ideas that are going to grab the attention of your clients and prospects, not to mention the media, your colleagues and other opinion formers.

It is the stage everyone wants to jump to. The fun brainstorming when we can call a meeting, get lots of flip charts up and do some creative thinking. But to work well, there are four stages and it is important you work through them systematically:

1. **Select the broad area of focus** for the project – for instance, is it going to focus on a particular sector, a particular challenge or event?

2. **Identify a specific theme or topic for researching** – following on from having decided the broad area of focus, you will need to target a specific area. On what topic do you want to develop attention-grabbing insights?

3. **Define the hypothesis** – this is the key part. You have to develop a hypothesis that, if confirmed, will provide an influential new perspective.

4. **Getting the evidence** – identify and provide the evidence you need to prove your hypothesis.

The first two are about deciding what area or topic to focus on, stages 3 and 4 are about creating the breakthrough insights and proving them.

You will note that the process is about you developing a hypothesis and then conducting research to prove it. We'll cover why this is the important formula as we go along.

Going through each of these carefully is key to a successful outcome: creating genuinely interesting and distinctive ideas that you can ultimately use to sell more services. Jumping through them can lead to disappointing outcomes or, nearly as bad, great thought leadership that does nothing for your business.

CHAPTER 9

Creating breakthrough ideas

This is the longest chapter in the book and completing it involves covering a lot of ground as we will be selecting an area of focus for your thought leadership initiative, a particular theme and then creating a specific hypothesis.

This approach of starting broad and getting narrow is important as creativity works best where there are clear parameters (not limitations!).

Many people may find this is not how they imagined it. Creativity to some is all about lots of ideas floating around followed by sudden inspiration in the shower or while walking the dog.

In fact, the better you can define the problem and the area for focus, the easier it is to apply your creativity.

Don't believe me? I will give a quick example. Have a try at writing a poem quickly, right now…

It is quite a hard task. You will generate questions and look for guidance about how long, what subject, what purpose. We all know what a poem is, but it is just too broad a request. Most people will struggle to get started.

Now try writing a poem, but this one has tight parameters. It needs to be about a man called Bob, who was a bit of a slob. It needs five lines, with the first, second and fifth lines rhyming with each other, and they can be a bit longer than the third and fourth lines. In other words, a limerick.

Now the job gets much easier. Ideas may already be coming thick and fast. But it was not different from the original task – after all, you could have created a limerick for that task originally.

So it is with your thought leadership initiative. If you are not focusing your efforts you will hit the same problems as with the unfocused poem-writing task.

In this book, the approach to overcoming this problem is to create that focus and structure, in stages, starting with deciding the broad area where you want to become a thought leader, and then narrowing until you have created a strong hypothesis that, if proven, will create breakthrough ideas.

However, what is also important is the human factor. If a subject scores highly, but the hearts of you and your team aren't in it, then it is never likely that you will find the passion to stay the course. Similarly, if you have a pet subject, and developing it clearly produces benefits for your business, this is the one you are most likely to pursue with energy and commitment.

Stage 1 – Selecting the broad area or topic for your thought leadership

OK, so we're clear that sensible boundaries and parameters will help in your creative process.

The first one you are going to decide is the broad area where you are going to focus your attention.

For instance:

- We want to be known for our expertise in the financial services sector, so it must relate to this.

- The firm is keen to get more corporate clients, so it must be relevant to them.

- We are a tax practice, so it must relate to tax in some form.

- Implementing workplace pensions is a big challenge to our clients at the moment and we want projects here, so it must relate to this.

Whether you have several competing areas or one sole contender, you should start to assess these broad areas based on three factors:

1. Where are the areas in your markets with the best opportunities for your business?

2. How well placed is your organisation (knowledge, services, capabilities, availability of key people, willingness to be involved, etc) to make an initiative in this area succeed?

3. Any other major internal political considerations at your organisation that could affect the choice of projects?

As summarised in the chart on page 111, you will normally want to concentrate your efforts on areas of high benefit but low risk, which generally will be areas where you have strong knowledge and experience that you can build on.

Certainly for your first thought leadership initiative, you really want to make it a success. Go for your strongest areas to give yourself the best chance.

Areas of low benefit probably will not justify the effort; while for areas of high benefit where you are weak you should build your knowledge before leaping into a major project.

There is plenty of scope for doing interesting thought leadership around theoretical issues, but most firms will be looking to have a strong sales return on their investment – and for that there needs to be an implicit link between the problem and services the firm can offer to tackle it.

However, firms with established thought leadership programmes can take a broader approach. For instance, at Accenture an important part of its programme is simply around relationship building.

Peter Thomas, Accenture's UK head of marketing, says: "Thought leadership positions a company around a topic that is interesting, market relevant and clients and other influencers want to read, delivered in a form they can digest.

"Our service lines produce thought leadership that speaks on important issues for their markets. By contrast, the Accenture Institute produces a lot of great thought leadership on major strategic issues that is not closely aligned to our service lines as this puts us in a position to get into dialogues with CEOs at the world's largest companies.

"My advice for businesses that are relatively new to thought leadership is to start with developing compelling and interesting points of view aligned with your firm's strategy and particular services."

If you have a number of competing areas, have a systematic way of assessing the best for your firm. Steve Blundell, of professional firm strategy consultancy Redstone Consultants, says: "We often score the applicability of a theme on a matrix with sectors, work types and jurisdictions to see which topics have the widest appeal or the biggest impact on a particular area."

This is important, as it is tempting to grab a theme because it is easy or one you like, but ultimately won't take you in the direction you want your business to go. For example, marketing consultant Ian Brodie recounts a problem he encountered through not aligning his activity with his strategy. He says: "When starting out on a project, you need to ask yourself: 'If it were a success, where would it lead?'

"One mistake I made was strongly promoting myself around business networking. I got lots of attention and I had lots of requests to speak on the subject. But actually it wasn't an area of interest to me, I had just done it opportunistically.

"In fact, I wanted to be getting leads and invitations on email marketing, not networking, so I had to stop it and start rebuilding my reputation in this area."

All of the above points are really important – you need to assess ideas to make sure they are genuinely going to help your firm. However, there is a big BUT that you need to bear in mind: the people factor. Ultimately, if an issue scores really highly but it simply doesn't 'float the boat' of anyone, there just won't be the enthusiasm needed to make it a success. Whatever idea you decide on, make sure there is someone who is really *committed* to making it a success.

Mapping the best areas for thought leadership for your organisation

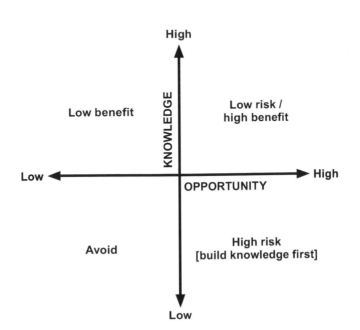

Find the best areas for your organisation's thought leadership

Proposed areas of broad focus	Opportunity Part 1 How big is the opportunity?	Opportunity Part 2 Can we deliver?	How strong is our knowledge in this area?	Is it a priority for us for thought leadership?

FOR EXAMPLE:				
Online credit card fraud against SMEs	**Low opportunity** It is a large but declining problem and there is strong competition.	**Strong** We have a small but highly proactive team.	**Very good** Our team not only does a lot of work in this area but also presents training courses and writes articles.	**Medium** Would be executed successfully, but it is not yet clear if it can lead to sufficient sales. **Action** Pursue if low-budget opportunities arise.
Current implementation of workplace pension requirements	**Large** It is a key part of our firm's growth strategy (as most UK organisations are implementing workplace pensions, or will soon have to).	**Strong** We have built up a strong team but there are insufficient leads and projects to keep them deployed at the moment. They are keen to do marketing initiatives.	**Extremely strong** Many of the team have been involved in the issue of workplace pensions for much of their career.	**High Action** Given timescale, need to pursue projects that can be implemented within next four months.

Why not do thought leadership to grow the business in an area of current weakness?

Shouldn't we do a project to help us in an area where we are weak but there is a lot of opportunity?

Sounds great in theory, but real-world problems from this thinking (which I frequently encounter) include:

- Without strong knowledge you are unlikely to develop anything exciting to say, and even if you do, you won't know whether it is exciting or mundane through weak knowledge.

- Your people will be too nervous of using it for fear of being exposed to questioning that will expose the lack of depth of their knowledge.

It's not impossible, and bringing in outside experts and consultants will plug knowledge gaps.

But I don't recommend it unless you do so much thought leadership that you are happy with the risk of the occasional failure.

Doing research and other initiatives to build your knowledge of important but weak areas may be a good thing for you to do. But you'll need to build your 'thought leadership muscles' before you are creating ideas that you can confidently deploy with knowledgeable clients and prospects.

Stage 2 – Identifying a great topic for your thought leadership

Part 1 – Background research

You and at least some of your team need to have good background knowledge of the area you have identified for developing a thought leadership initiative, not least because you are going to have to brainstorm and assess ideas quite early in the process.

Sounds common sense that people involved in creating breakthrough insights should have a really strong knowledge of the area. The reality is that employees get roped into projects and their knowledge isn't great because the programme takes them from areas of comfort (their professional expertise) into new areas.

A good exercise to do with the team involved in the project is to have a brainstorm on 'what would you expect an expert on this subject to know?' Afterwards make sure you know everything on that list, and make sure your team is doing the same too; the more knowledgeable the team, the better the end result.

Here are some of the things you and your team can do to immerse yourselves quickly:

1. Subscribe to, and read (!) the trade publications that cover this market/topic.

2. Set up a Google Alert for the topic.

3. Identify who publishes good research. Subscribe to it.

4. Identify other advisers and suppliers who are active in this sector (not just your rivals, but all sorts of suppliers). Subscribe to their newsletters and marketing.

5. Identify *Financial Times* and other journalists who cover this subject. Set up alerts on the *FT* and other websites to get the articles they write.

6. Read some books on the subject.

7. Are there any relevant TED talks? If so, listen to them.

8. Worried you will have too much reading? Appoint someone in your team to do a weekly digest of important developments and further reading.

9. Look online for sector-specific networking and discussion events. Go to them!

10. Identify key events for the sector (exhibitions, conferences, etc). Attend!

11. Anything else you and your team can think of.

It sounds a lot. It shouldn't be if it is an area that interests you. In a few months' time you will be launching yourself on the world as an expert, and it is not unreasonable for your clients and prospects to expect you to be well read on the subject.

Similarly, later you will want to know if your ideas are credible and interesting. To answer that question you need to be knowledgeable and able to debate your ideas with people who don't agree with you.

Part 2 – Finding a killer topic

This stage is where the fun brainstorming can start and is all about deciding a topic for your thought leadership. From this will come a specific hypothesis that you will seek to prove.

The process is NOT about doing lots of research and hoping you will come across an interesting trend no one has noticed before – that is like looking for the proverbial needle in a haystack. It is about creating a really interesting hypothesis and then seeking to prove it.

The first two stages will mean you can now focus on areas of strength and opportunity for your business, with all the main participants having at least the sort of basic knowledge that will allow them to contribute. However, there is also a good argument

The process is NOT about doing lots of research and hoping you will come across an interesting trend no one has noticed before – that is like looking for the proverbial needle in a haystack. It is about creating a really interesting hypothesis and then seeking to prove it.

for including a few people who are unfamiliar with the subject as naïve questions can often lead to great fresh avenues of thought.

You may already have a very firm idea of the theme you want your thought leadership project to be about. If so, you can jump to stage 3: creating a powerful hypothesis – on page 126.

If not, I am going to introduce you to some great exercises to allow you and your team to identify areas of interest – both to you and your clients.

Great areas for thought leadership

Whichever technique you use in identifying your theme, great areas for thought leadership are those where:

- There are changes taking place rapidly and businesses are struggling to keep pace; and/or

- There are changes going to happen, and those likely to be affected have yet to realise this or do not appreciate the implications; and/or

- There is an absence of important information; and/or

- You believe the perceived wisdom to be outdated or otherwise suspect.

- You are likely to be in a position to suggest practical steps to tackling the problem or opportunity identified.

Option 1 - Kelso Ideas Circles

My favourite approach, which works well for brainstorms to decide the areas of focus, is nicknamed the Kelso Ideas Circles (or Kick, as we use it to kick out ideas that won't deliver and home in on ones that will).

Typically, you and your team brainstorm three broad areas to identify those subjects that tick all the boxes. The three areas are:

1 – Megatrends. These are the big tectonic issues affecting your clients and their sector. They are typically very important but slow-moving issues that may have been around for a while and certainly will be important in a few years too. Examples might include such things as: ageing population; rise of Chinese middle class; mobile commerce; the 'internet of things'; regulatory burden; and ethical consumerism.

This is a great way to start the brainstorm with as it moves people's mindset from short-term tactical sales issues to a broader strategic perspective.

2 – Hot topics. This is the opposite sort of issue. These are issues that are coming up and will be of concern for a limited period. Examples include new laws and regulations (and their implementation dates); current court cases; external events that will have a big impact or are important for sales.

It should also include major recurring events that have an impact (for instance: Christmas for retailers and post-Christmas sales for holiday companies; 'bonus season' for the City).

You might also include Donald Rumsfeld-esque 'known unknowns' – things you know will probably happen, but you don't know the timing or the form. Examples of this are hostile takeovers and major cyber-attacks/data loss; or perhaps prosecutions by the Financial Conduct Authority (FCA).

If these are a big prospect in your sector you should include them. While you don't know when or who, you can take the view that they are highly likely or even inevitable over the next year.

3 – Industry-specific (or theme-specific). For this one you brainstorm and list any other areas relevant to the industry sector or theme on which you are focusing that don't fit into the other two categories.

The next bit is the important part. You create a Venn diagram of three circles (as in the diagram below) and place the outcomes of your brainstorm in their relevant positions in circles. Ideally do this with the group after the brainstorm.

The important bit is to find themes that fall in areas of overlap between the three circles. The 'best' themes are those that fall in the middle, where all three overlap. Here's why…

Megatrends are great areas for thought leadership. They are big, important and will be relevant for a long while. Your thought leadership on them will have a long shelf life, and a long-term positioning as an expert on this theme will be a valuable and enduring asset.

However, such themes can also be bland, theoretical and lack immediacy.

Topicality is the opposite. It is immediate, people are thinking about it, they need to act. It is a great theme for getting attention, sales and press coverage. But once it has happened, your theme is gone and your intellectual capital redundant.

The ideal opportunity (the centre point of the Kelso Ideas Circles) is generally the best place for your thought leadership. These are themes that are part of a megatrend, and which will have a strong and impending impact on your clients and prospects.

Kelso Ideas Circle (Kick)
Is your theme in the magic centre spot?

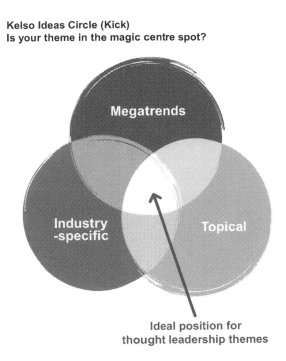

Ideal position for
thought leadership themes

Afterwards, you should assess these themes against areas of strength and weakness for your organisation using the chart on page 121.

Strong areas, where you are knowledgeable and have relevant services so you are in a good position to help your clients, are great places for thought leadership. You have good foundations there and can convert the investment of time and money into sales.

Weak areas you kick out, at least as far as the thought leadership project is concerned. But don't lose them. You now also have a list of important areas for your clients where your firm is weak and has nothing to offer.

This may be alarming! If there are big areas affecting your clients you will want to develop knowledge and offerings to help them, but that is a separate issue to thought leadership where you want to major on areas of strength and opportunity.

Kick results

Record your Kick results in a table along the following lines:

Theme / idea from Kick	Do we have strong knowledge relevant to this particular area?	Do we have services that help us tackle this problem (or can we develop them)?	Any other reasons why this is either a good area for us or a difficult one?

Option 2 - SWOT and PEST analyses

Generally ideas come thick and fast when using Kick, although I always come armed with a few suggestions to 'get the ball rolling' as some teams can be reticent to offer up the first suggestions if they have not done much of this before.

In fact, typically the response is that afterwards teams involved say it is hugely useful for them to look at clients from this strategic perspective, and they wish they did more of it.

If you feel something stronger is needed to cover as wide a range of themes as possible, then SWOT and PEST analyses are great. You can take their outcomes and use the chart above to assess them according to the Kick criteria.

SWOT and PEST analyses

These are great tools to use, particularly at the outset, to get your team thinking broadly about the big issues of the challenge. A SWOT is better for challenges that are more tightly defined.

For instance, if you have decided your thought leadership project is going to look at a challenge facing retailers, you could start with a PEST on the sector as a whole and the big issues it faces.

However, maybe you have already decided that you want to look at a particular regulatory change affecting retailers. You would then use the SWOT to look at this area in more detail.

A SWOT analysis, as described in Wikipedia, is a structured *planning* method used to evaluate the strengths, weaknesses, opportunities and threats involved in a *project* or *business* venture.

Doing a SWOT is one of the most common management tools, and in it you brainstorm each of its four categories:

- **Strengths:** characteristics of the business or other group that give it an advantage over others.

- **Weaknesses:** characteristics that place the business or group at a disadvantage relative to others.

- **Opportunities:** elements that the group (or members of it) could exploit to its advantage.

- **Threats:** elements in the environment that could cause trouble for these businesses.

Another approach is the PEST analysis, which takes the same approach to look at the big issues affecting businesses and other groups. The factors are:

- Political

- Economic

- Social

- Technological

In a sign of the times, it has been expanded since my days at university to STEEPLED to also include:

- Legal

- Environmental

- Ethics

- Demographics

Getting brainstorms right

Here's the best way to have a brainstorm. You have one or two senior people and several junior ones in the session. The senior ones spend their time criticising and generally shooting down the suggestions of others. The meeting continues until the first half-decent sounding idea emerges, and everyone latches on to this.

OK, that's a poor way of doing brainstorms – but surprisingly commonplace nonetheless.

There are lots of guides online and in print on successful brainstorm meetings and you should look at these.

It is important to think of who will be at the brainstorm, and the political and personal chemistry that will be present.

For instance, senior professionals can often railroad or stifle a meeting. If your team isn't used to thinking outside of their professional 'box' (frequently the case), without a great facilitator, you will probably get groupthink and little originality.

If your team is big enough, consider having senior and junior people tackle the same problem. Also include lively thinkers from elsewhere in the firm as they can ask provocative 'naïve' questions that uncover hidden assumptions and lead to new insights.

Robert Pay, the business development director of international management consultants Alvarez & Marsal, says: "Brainstorming effectively is key for consultants, and we utilise a whole range of techniques. One tip is to make the process a bit competitive. For instance, we often get groups in different countries to tackle the same topic in order to get a range of different perspectives – with each team aiming to have the best ideas."

Option 3 - Mind Mapping the big issues from your brainstorms

If your brainstorms have left you with lots of issues, but no structure, a good way to untangle your thoughts so you can focus is to Mind Map them. An example of this is below, showing a brainstorm on major trends affecting the legal sector.

Example mapped output from brainstorm – legal sector trends

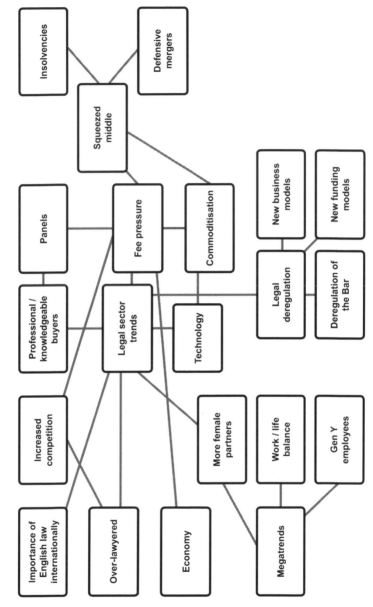

From the Mind Map, if inspiration is not jumping out, highlight areas where:

- There are changes taking place rapidly and people are struggling to keep pace; and/or

- There are changes going to happen, and people have yet to realise this or do not appreciate their implications; and/or

- There is an absence of important information; and/or

- You think the perceived wisdom is outdated or otherwise suspect.

Stage 3 – Creating a powerful hypothesis that will bring breakthrough insights

In the previous stage you and your team will have identified topics where something interesting and important is happening. It is something that is very relevant to your clients, and they almost certainly don't realise the impact on them – and your business is well placed to help.

Having chosen this area, or maybe a shortlist of areas, the final stages are to:

1. Create a challenging thesis (a thesis is a statement that declares what you believe and what you intend to prove).

2. Set about proving (or disproving) this hypothesis.

This may be a surprise to you – seeking to create the insights *before* any research, not afterwards.

I cannot overstate the importance of starting with a strong hypothesis (an interesting, relevant and challenging or counterintuitive viewpoint) so you know from the outset what you want to find or prove.

If you have time for the alternative, undertaking lots of analysis and original research on this topic to see what eventually emerges, that is great. However, it could take a long while and, even if you do find something of interest, it may be in an area that is not hugely relevant to the services your business provides. In other words, you may have ended up creating great research on problems that you can't help solve.

Once you have a hypothesis, by contrast, you are then in the right position to decide what evidence you need to support it and how to obtain it, focusing your efforts greatly. You also know in advance if it is going to be an interesting and attention-grabbing discovery if you prove it (and if not, you can save yourself the bother of looking!).

> Once you have a hypothesis you are then in the right position to decide what evidence you need to support it and how to obtain it – focusing your efforts greatly.

Coming up with the thesis can be a challenge, although it may have leapt out during the earlier brainstorms.

If not, ways you might go about creating it, other than simply waiting for inspiration, are:

1. You do a survey of senior people in the sector, asking lots of questions while hoping that some will hit the mark and identify a surprise (not a recommended approach).

2. You brainstorm and perhaps also use a few creativity techniques to generate an interesting thesis.

3. You conduct a short series of in-depth interviews (typically, but not necessarily, with senior people in the sector) with the aim of getting deep understanding and identifying areas or approaches in common.

The first option – surveys where people go out fishing for ideas – is not to be recommended. Why? Reasons include:

- First, it almost certainly won't work. Lots of questions that fish for an interesting area is typically a sign of desperation. And if you are lucky to find something from the exercise, you almost certainly won't have asked questions that are specific enough to get the sort of detail needed. Unless you have the budget for a second round of more detailed research, avoid such 'fishing' surveys.

- Second, people mistake these surveys for proper thought leadership. Because the survey has taken a lot of effort, and perhaps has been costly too, they end up publishing it. But such surveys typically bring little by way of insight as a broad area is covered so insufficient detail is generated.

These sorts of report, where the firm started without a thesis, are easy to spot as you find lots of charts and tables of data but no insights. They often happen when the task is dumped on the marketing team, which is then given insufficient senior involvement. The subsequent report will almost certainly have a counterproductive impact by showing to recipients that the firm has nothing of interest to say on the subject!

What should your hypothesis say?

At its simplest it should:

- Cover an area of importance or topicality.

- Tackle a problem, cost, misconception or missed opportunity that is causing, or will cause, significant problems for your target audience.

- If proven, lead to the revelation that businesses (or other parties, such as regulators, government, employees, etc) need to alter their opinions and behaviour.

Your hypothesis could be one that challenges industry wisdom or otherwise throws previously unknown insights or detail on to an important area.

Creating powerful hypotheses

Sometimes your hypothesis will be obvious from the brainstorm and Kick analysis you have already done. However, usually you and your team will need to work at it a bit. Below are two approaches that work really well.

The key to them is they go beyond looking at the impact on clients; they seek to look at the impact on the stakeholders that matter to clients, such as their customers, employees, shareholders and/or regulators.

1 – Asking the 'right' questions

The first approach is to simply ask the *right* questions. You have to be a ruthless interrogator and not give up asking until you get to the 'right' answer.

Generally, the questioning needs to start at the theme you have identified and the changes taking place. You then follow these changes through to unravel their impact by continuing to ask such questions as: "What will their impact be on X stakeholder?" "Who are the winners and losers?" and "What changes will this cause?"

It is a matter of not stopping at what the immediate impact will be on your clients, but asking what the impact will be on their important stakeholders – whether employees, customers, suppliers, competitors, investors. How will their behaviour change and what will be the implications of this (whether opportunities or challenges)?

2 – Identifying all the winners and losers

An alternative approach is to start with identifying the groups that will be winners and losers. There is nothing that grabs people's attention like the prospect of being harmed, or indeed the prospect of there being an opportunity.

Don't just stop at the obvious ones but work through who will lose as the trend or changes you have identified start to happen. Work through the impact, whether it is on markets, countries, population sectors, or individuals in particular income or demographic bands.

Use this chart to record the stages as you work through creating the outline hypothesis

The broad area of focus for our thought leadership is (from Kick, Pest or Swot):	
The trends we have identified are:	
What will each of these trends mean for businesses in this market?	
Who are the main stakeholders of our clients and prospects?	
What will be the impact of these trends on each stakeholder group – and on stakeholders' behaviour?	
Who are the likely winners and losers from these trends?	
The hypothesis emerging is:	

An example hypothesis

For instance, here is one from a project I am working on with a client at the time of writing this book.

This project looks at new changes proposed by the Chancellor of the Exchequer in 2014 that will give pensioners greater access to their pension fund (so when they retire they won't have to buy an annuity, and will seemingly have much greater leeway over where they invest this money, or perhaps simply spend it).

This subject is very topical and is an area where my client wants to be seen as a 'go-to' expert, reflecting their intention of becoming leading commentators on the laws facing people who have been mis-sold investments.

Our main hypothesis is that a sizeable group of adults in the 40-70 age range do not have the financial acumen to invest such large sums wisely. This challenges the government's view that people are the best judges here. The implication is that many will ultimately face impoverishment later in retirement and needlessly become a financial burden on the taxpayer and on their family.

We have various sub-hypotheses. For instance: people won't trust banks but will be unclear who they *can* trust with their investments, leaving them vulnerable to the unscrupulous. Also, we suggest that people will choose to spend a chunk enjoying an active early retirement, unaware about how big its impact will be on their future pension income.

In this case our main hypothesis works regardless for any reasonably likely outcome. We aren't saying that the majority of people will be vulnerable, just that a sizeable group will be, and our research aims to quantify it and bring insight into the problems arising from this and their implications.

As an aside, while preparing the survey we were beaten to the punch on one of the main themes (people will spend too much of their pension fund). As with all our surveys, we had ensured that there were several themes, so with slight adjustments, the project continued as planned. It is always worth having more than one hypothesis you want to prove; the reality is a lot of firms do thought leadership and someone else is almost certainly working on the same subject at the same time as you!

Example development of hypothesis

In the example on the following page the team moves from a broad area of interest (challenges facing mid-sized retailers) through the output of their brainstorm, to a very specific hypothesis regarding market opportunities arising from our ageing population.

Example development of hypothesis

The area of focus for our thought leadership is:	The challenges facing mid-sized retailers in an increasingly competitive market
What are the major trends affecting retailers?	Online shopping, home delivery and 'the death of the high street'? Environmental and sustainability concerns Food provenance and food chain concerns Concern over waste of unsold food Smaller 'big chain' stores in high streets Ageing population Population moving to cities Potential for using apps on customers' smartphones Impact of business rates More home working
What will these trends mean for our retail clients (especially with regard to our area of focus)?	**Example:** the ageing population means there is a large and growing market segment with particular needs
Who are the main stakeholders of our clients and prospects?	Shoppers, employees, suppliers and investors
What will be the impact of these trends on each stakeholder group – and on stakeholders' behaviour?	**Shoppers:** more will be unable to get to supermarkets or will need assistance when in stores **Employees:** may need training in helping elderly customers correctly **Suppliers:** products need to be suitable for elderly customers
What hypothesis is emerging?	**Example:** The large elderly market is a missed opportunity for many grocery retailers because of hard-to-read labels, impossible-to-open packaging, cavernous and badly located stores, and staff who are too busy to help. It offers huge potential for retailers who can adapt to their needs.

Fire-proofing your hypothesis

OK. You have your hypothesis, all you need to do is prove it, and that is what we'll be doing in the next chapter.

But first of all you should sense-check it for two elements:

- Is your hypothesis plausible (as you don't want to spend a lot of time researching something only to find you are wrong)?

- Is your hypothesis, if proven, going to be genuinely interesting?

To ensure your hypothesis is indeed going to lead to genuine thought leadership you should do the following (especially the fourth one as a safety net – there are plenty of cases where people launch into research sure of the answer, only to find the results confounded their expectations):

1 – Peer review

Make sure you get feedback early on from knowledgeable people who will 'speak truth to power'. Your colleagues are a good starting point, so discuss your hypothesis with them. You don't need a consensus from them, but they are a useful sounding board and source of insight and challenge.

2 – Ask clients

Many people want to keep their thought leadership under tight wraps, unveiling it only once it is totally complete. This prevents the huge benefit of using others to develop your thoughts and bring informed independent challenges. I strongly suggest discussing your hypothesis with some trusted clients and see what their views are.

3 – Have evidence

Have you already identified credible evidence that could indicate your hypothesis is right? What has been written about this specific matter recently that supports your views?

4 – Have alternative angles if the research does not go as expected

The best subjects are those where you can have something interesting to say whatever the outcome of the research.

Work through your hypothesis and make sure you consider how you can have an interesting angle for alternative outcomes:

1. Your hypothesis is proven.

2. Your hypothesis is disproven.

3. The research is equivocal (and doesn't prove or disprove the hypothesis).

By this point you should be in a really strong position: a credible hypothesis on an area of strong interest to your target audience that if proven will allow you to engage with them, ultimately promoting your ability to help them tackle this problem or opportunity.

You have taken all reasonable steps to make sure your ideas are likely and will be of interest, and you've thought about what you can say if, to everyone's surprise, evidence suggests your hypothesis isn't correct and something else is in fact the case.

The next step is to prove your hypothesis so you can get on with the desired outcome: a high-profile campaign unveiling your ideas.

CHAPTER 10

Proving your hypothesis

The essential step that turns your ideas into thought leadership gold dust is getting credible evidence that proves your hypothesis.

A great idea that lacks supporting evidence is simply conjecture. It is not compelling, no matter how much you may believe that it is true.

Having created a great hypothesis that, when proven, will turn the heads of your clients and prospects, we now need to identify what evidence is needed to support it.

That is not to say you must get every bit of evidence, nor does it mean that every bit of evidence will support your hypothesis. What it does mean is that you will have made a conscious choice whether to seek it or not; you will make a conscious choice whether to look at it; and, most important of all, you know this information should you get challenged on it later.

The process is to work out what evidence you need to substantiate it (and perhaps also to refute alternatives).

My approach is to ask: "If the hypothesis is correct, how would it be evident?" For instance, would people behave in a particular way, would people hold particular views, would certain financial or other measurements reflect it, etc?

Once we know what we are trying to identify, it is a case of finding the best sources of evidence to substantiate this.

Immediately below is an example chart you can use for working through the process with your hypothesis (downloadable from www.kelsopr.com/thought-leadership-manual-resources), and later in the chapter is a chart summarising the types of evidence you may look for and its pros and cons.

Our hypothesis is: (add hypothesis here)				
	If it is the case, how would it be evident?	How would we identify and quantify this change?	What sources could we use?	What types of evidence do we need?
1				
2				
3				
4				
5				

Types of evidence for supporting your hypothesis

In terms of evidence to support your hypothesis, on the following page is a summary of the principal sources of evidence to show that it is correct (or that may contradict it).

Generally, you will want to use as many as possible to maximise the amount of evidence that your hypothesis is correct.

Getting credible support for your hypothesis is essential. If you do a survey, the research may well end up as the largest cost for the project, so let's look at the options in more detail.

Evidence for your breakthrough insights – a summary

Type of evidence	Pros	Cons	Comment
Client case studies	Very compelling evidence and marketing tool; highlights first-hand knowledge	Getting agreement from some organisations can be difficult	'Show me where this is happening' is going to be the first question most people will have
Public domain examples	A great proof point	If you don't know the business, your insights will be limited	Being able to cite actual examples (clients and in the market broadly) will normally be essential
Endorsements from credible people (for your views)	Very compelling to have people like senior executives backing your views	Have to make sure it is seen as your insight (not theirs)	There is nothing like independent support for your views from credible, senior people
Analysis of your own internal data	Very powerful where reliable data is available	Most firms overlook doing this. Requires a large sample base	There is a huge opportunity for firms to make more use of their own data
Analysis of external data	Usually cheap/free. Immediately available. Provides data you cannot create yourself	No real drawbacks, except that you are limited by what is available	A huge amount of data is available for free or at little cost. Make as much use of it as you can
Opinion surveys	You decide the questions and criteria. Omnibus surveys can be cost-effective	Can be expensive. Better for providing evidence than insight	A powerful tool. Perhaps overused
Calculations and worked examples	Really show the impact. Usually cheap/free. Appears scientific	None (other than people don't do enough of it)!	Powerful, but keep it simple and relevant. Ensure you create a headline figure
Freedom of Information requests	Cheap. Official = credible. Looks like you have forced a revelation of hidden data!	Limited to data held by public bodies. Responses may take a long time or be refused	FoI requests are a powerful way of adding impact. Use them whenever you can

Defining the evidence you need – a worked example

So, how does this work in practice? On the following page I have a worked example using the project from the previous chapter (from page 131), where I was helping my client develop a project around the theme of people losing their pension fund (when the government gives them greater control on what they do with it).

There are a couple of points to highlight with the example of the previous page:

- In the third and fourth columns they note that using and reviewing existing data is important. This will invariably be the case for you, and we look at using existing data further in Chapters 11 and 12.

- The second point to note is that, in this case, it is a new subject and on many of the issues there is a strong need to ask and test people, which has driven this example strongly down the opinion survey route (which is indeed what we did on this project).

However, beware! A lot of people automatically jump to the conclusion that they need to do an opinion poll or some other sort of survey. Don't make this assumption; there are plenty of occasions where opinion polls and surveys are not appropriate, and other forms of evidence, such as desk research, analysis or case studies, are better. We look at them in more detail in the following chapter as getting the research right is essential for the accuracy and credibility of your campaign.

Worked example: research needed for pensions thought leadership campaign

Our hypothesis is:
A sizeable group of adults in the 40-70 age range do not have the financial acumen to invest such large sums wisely

	If it is the case, how would it be evident?	How would we identify and quantify this?	What sources could we use?	What types of evidence do we need?	Next steps and timescale (to identify specific sources)	Who is doing it?
1	Can people answer basic financial questions?	Ask them	Existing research Give people a test	Analysis of existing data Survey people and ask / test them		
2	Do people have experience of investing large sums?	Ask them	Existing research Ask them	Identify existing research and/or survey people		
3	Would they spend too much of it?	Ask them Find out what do they do with the existing £100k allowed from their pension	Existing research Ask retired people what they did, and those about to retire what they will do	Identify existing research and/or survey people		
4	Is there evidence of comparable situations elsewhere?	What happens in other countries? What do people do with other large lump sums?	Research the situation in other countries Look for existing research	Data on problems arising in relevant countries		
5	Evidence of people losing their pensions through poor investments or unscrupulous people	My client's cases National data on this problem	Case studies Analysis of cases Research public bodies for data	Case studies Identify data from public bodies (or make a Freedom of Information request)		

CHAPTER 11

Getting your research right

In this chapter we are going to go through the principal sources of evidence to prove your hypothesis.

As with other sections of this book, I'm not going to provide a '*How to do Research 101*' guide; the assumption is that either you have some familiarity or you'll get a more detailed guide for particular aspects.

For instance, to analyse data you will want to be familiar with Excel; there are enough guides on Excel for there to be no need for me to go through this. However, what I will be doing is highlighting a few tips and other aspects relevant to our goal: creating strong thought leadership that will grab the attention of your clients.

I am also going to take the opportunity to reiterate a point I made earlier: thought leadership does not equal doing surveys. Surveys are fantastic and I use them a lot with our clients. But you should aim to find out absolutely the maximum you can from other sources, and use surveys as a last, not first, resort.

In fact, it is vital to be able to substantiate your hypothesis, turning it from speculation to insight. Ways of doing this include:

Case studies and public domain examples

Being able to support your hypothesis by saying "… and here is an example of it happening" is hugely powerful.

This could be done with case studies of your clients, case studies of businesses that aren't your clients and simply using examples already in the public domain.

Their benefit is that, if done well, a case study is powerful and compelling as subsequent marketing and sales material, as well as supporting your thought leadership.

It provides evidence of the issues at hand as well as demonstrating and endorsing your ability to tackle it successfully.

A case study should be a drama of success despite adversity and tribulation, while in a world of assertion and generalisation it can provide much-needed specifics and context.

In fact, there is also nothing business people like more than reading how their peers have overcome challenges similar to those they face. It helps them learn the lessons and avoid the pitfalls.

Sadly, most case studies don't deliver this, simply being anonymised stories of 'wonderful company brings in wonderful supplier and things go wonderfully without the slightest hitch, delivering even more wonderful results'. If only life were like that!

Of course, a balancing act needs to be achieved. No company will thank you for publishing a case study that makes them look foolish, and there is nothing that will wind up your readers more than you implying 'smart consultants know far more than their clients and save the day once again'.

Elsewhere in the book we look at the importance of getting your clients involved in the thought leadership process, and the benefits this brings all concerned.

Tips for including case studies in your thought leadership:

- At the outset, get your most senior person to deal directly with the most senior person you can. If it is agreed at the top, it is much more likely to happen.

- Often the biggest hurdle is getting your own people to approach the client! Some businesses are great, but at others people seem scared and go about it the wrong way (or won't do it at all). If this is your business, there is extra help among the resources at www.kelsopr.com/thought-leadership-manual-resources

- With owner-managed businesses, getting agreement for a case study is straightforward. You simply ask the owner or one of the senior leadership team. With large organisations or where you don't deal with the senior team, it can get harder. Their corporate communications departments may well get involved and they are typically the kiss of death.

  Big companies get hundreds of requests from suppliers for case studies and many have a policy of automatically saying no. Those that don't reject them out of hand will treat them as a pretty low priority that offers few benefits for them and their business but plenty of downsides. If you are running into this problem, there is also help on this at www.kelsopr.com/thought-leadership-manual-resources

All of the above applies to public domain examples (that is, examples that illustrate your hypothesis, but where you weren't involved). This isn't necessarily a problem and your main choices are:

1. Utilise the example, using information that is in the public domain (and not inform the company); or

2. Approach the company and ask for its involvement in your research (eg an interview, etc). The advantage with this approach is that you will invariably get additional insights, and you build up contacts at a potential prospect too. Quite frankly, I would recommend doing this wherever possible – the business will be flattered and who knows where the new relationship will lead?

Case studies – start them early!

With case studies, it is important to start on them well in advance. You will be working to a timescale, but getting people to agree to take part, find time and, on top of that, approve comments, can take many months.

---

2 - Data analysis – external data sources

There is a vast amount of data available freely or at low cost. It is a huge resource that you should make as much use of as possible to add impact and credibility to your thought leadership.

Some of it comes from the many public and private organisations that publish statistics, ranging from the National Statistics Office through survey companies through to investment banks, trade associations and member organisations to Companies House and a whole range of business data providers.

Useful thought leadership data sources

For a list of sources of really useful data, go to
www.kelsopr.com/thought-leadership-manual-resources

The benefits of making use of existing data include:

1. Reviewing and incorporating existing data is generally cheap and low risk (much is available publicly or at low cost, removing the risk of paying for something that doesn't help you).

2. It gives independent corroboration (assuming it supports your view; if it doesn't, you need to know in case of challenges).

3. It allows you to focus your thought leadership on new insights (not covering old ground).

4. If it is not recent, you can still use it to highlight the trend (eg 'Research two years ago found X, but now the situation is Y').

With all these benefits, make as much use of existing research as you can, and then build on it.

You should make as much use of this huge resource as possible within your thought leadership, and ways include:

- **Identifying published research that supports your hypothesis.** For research that doesn't, you should identify this too as you will need to tackle it. Ask yourself if it is current, if it is rigorous, are its implications open to interpretation, in what way is it less credible than yours… or do you need to rethink your hypothesis?

- **Use it to scale up your research to give sector and 'UK PLC' figures.** If you want to get PR, then often you will need to include a 'cost to UK PLC' – ie what is the cost to the country? This is a very powerful statistic for PR purposes (often essential). To scale up your finding to give it national impact you usually need to bring in data from public bodies.

- For instance, to calculate the cost of a change affecting medium businesses, if you can estimate the average cost for an SME then data from the National Statistics Office will allow you to scale up your figure across the whole country by multiplying it by the number of mid-sized businesses.

- **Combining data from different sources to provide evidence** – such as charts, scattergrams, ratios or all sorts of other ways of reusing it.

  For example, Accenture is a master of using other organisations' data as part of its thought leadership. You often see calculations billed as 'Accenture Research' but when you drill into the report, you find that much of the data comes from a number of other sources (including their rivals) but the firm has melded it together into its own calculation (getting the credit without having to go to the cost and effort of producing all the original data).

Once you get going, you will almost certainly find there is a lot of data out there – some of it very useful.

Research case studies – KPMG and BDO fraud reports

KPMG has a long-running quarterly *Fraud Barometer* looking at business fraud in the UK, and BDO introduced a similar one a decade or so ago.

In both cases the methodology revolves around searching online and through databases they subscribe to, using the key word 'fraud' or similar to identify all reported cases. After this the researcher goes to work, cataloguing each incident to form the database the report draws on.

First of all, it is a great example of thinking laterally and creatively about what data is needed and how the power of the internet can be used to create a data source you can use.

KPMG and BDO are big organisations with lots of resources, but even a small firm could apply this approach.

Research example – Begbies Traynor's Red Flag Alerts

An even better example of using existing data imaginatively is the Red Flag Alerts research created by insolvency and business recovery specialists Begbies Traynor.

This quarterly research, which got substantial coverage for the firm, used data from commercial information providers on the number and type of businesses in trouble – in this case details of county court judgments, winding-up petitions and voluntary arrangements. This was presented by industry sector and region, giving the firm distinctive insights on changes in the corporate health of UK SMEs – and very substantial press coverage for the firm every time it was published.

3 - Data analysis – using your own data

There are lots of big, nosey organisations gathering data on us all the time: Google, Facebook, the US government and GCHQ, to name but a few.

This is bad news in terms of our privacy but good news in terms of generating insights, as it's not just them. All sorts of businesses generate reams of data about their employees, their customers, their users and all sorts of other people. Once upon a time this was seen as a waste by-product. Now it is called big data and it is a huge resource.

Getting the most out of your own data

- Virtually every business has data lurking inside it (especially cloud-based and service businesses).

- It's typically free and this is a hugely valuable resource.

- When you have data it adds a whole new layer of credibility to you and your arguments.

- Don't just present your data, interpret it, highlighting trends your data illustrates.

- Mix your data with external sources to aggregate up 'UK PLC figures' for high-impact PR.

- Don't be too ambitious at the start. Keep it simple and build the scope and complexity with future versions.

Even if your company isn't collecting huge amounts of data through the various electronic touch points, it will have other insights gained through the projects and the other day-to-day work of its professionals and managers.

Whether through the website, through the cash till, through the IT centre, in the call centre, through surveys during recruitment, through online payments or the reports your people make on site, there is a huge and ever-growing amount of data to be used.

To demonstrate the power of your own data, especially when you are on a limited budget, here are two examples of smaller businesses I worked with (both campaigns subsequently won awards).

Using your own data to become the market leader – case study: GlobalExpense

GlobalExpense started in 2001 with three people and grew to 90 in 2011 (when it was acquired by a much larger overseas competitor).

It offered outsourced employee expenses management and was an early innovator in what were then called Application Service Providers and what are now referred to as cloud services.

It acquired many FTSE and other blue-chip clients, ultimately handling the expense claims of hundreds of thousands of their employees who would log into its software with a browser to fill out their expense claims (and to approve the claims of their subordinates).

This meant GlobalExpense had a vast amount of data from the millions of expense claims being entered.

For GlobalExpense this was a waste by-product, but once aggregated, anonymised, data mined and analysed, it was used to create the first ever annual employee expenses benchmarking report. This gave information on everything from the average expense claim for individual products, and their frequency, to whether VAT was being successfully reclaimed, split by such factors as business size and industry sector.

Through mixing with other data, we were then also able to estimate the amount of expenses fraud being committed by employees around the country and the total cost across the economy to British businesses each year.

The annual report was great for content marketing and generally positioning GlobalExpense as the leader in this new market. In fact, it not only became their main annual lead generation initiative, having the data proved particularly powerful for the firm's sales team, allowing them to win pitches for very large companies on the insights and challenges they were able to bring.

In other words, it allowed them to switch from selling on features and benefits to 'challenger selling', one of the latest buzzwords, well before the term was even coined. This approach even allowed them to beat bigger competitors (whose software was probably better), by enabling GlobalExpense to move the consideration at pitches on to an area in which it was strong – compliance.

In addition to positioning the firm strongly as market leader and allowing it to punch above its weight at pitches, it also ensured substantial coverage for the firm (far greater than a firm with under 100 people would normally expect), including all the quality national daily newspapers, with a mention on the front page of the *Financial Times* a particular highlight.

When other expenses-related stories were in the headlines (such as the MPs' expenses scandal of 2009), they were consequently approached to be expert commentators. While they knew little about MPs' expenses, they could talk about the situation facing the rest of us and how the rules in Parliament were completely at odds with the rest of the country.

David Vine, then CEO at GlobalExpense, said: "For our business development, the report was key. It was an excellent tool which was used on our website and by our sales teams out and about in the field. The report demonstrated that we invested heavily in our products, while gaining vital understanding and knowledge of the markets.

"For the sales team, the thought leadership report was their number one tool. The report was a very powerful asset to have because it set meetings off in the right direction and gave a strong position to sell from. It helps to be able to walk into a room knowing not only that you are the experts at what you do, but also to have the proof to back this up.

"None of our competitors at the time were producing anything like it. So it gave us a tremendous competitive edge and positioned us as the industry leader in the UK, allowing for the business ultimately to be sold very successfully to a leading international business."

All of this was achieved utilising data that was residing, largely unwanted, in the firm's systems (for PR purposes we also combined it with survey and government data too).

What data is captured, perhaps unknown and unloved, in your systems that can be utilised?

Using your data to open doors and grab the front page – case study

A smaller management consultancy client was keen to use a thought leadership campaign to open doors to senior people.

Its targets were chief executives at larger councils. In the past it had found it could use a telesales approach to secure meetings, but in recent years it had got much harder, to such an extent that in the past year no meetings had been achieved.

The firm, which specialises in improving the effectiveness of organisations by boosting the supervisory skills of managers and team leaders, had data from its many client projects going back over 15 years.

This was consolidated in Excel (much of it had previously been on paper), and I worked with them to analyse it and pull out headline-grabbing findings (in fact we knew the headline we wanted, it was a case of getting robust proof).

The report, based entirely on their first-hand experience from projects, generated substantial coverage, ranging from the front page of the *Daily Telegraph* and BBC Radio 4 to the local government trade press.

The report and coverage were then utilised in a direct marketing campaign, followed up by the telesales agency to secure meetings. It was a different story now; previously there had been no success, but this time around eight meetings were secured within the first few weeks.

This example is here to highlight that you don't have to be an online business to have lots of data; even professional firms doing it the old-school way with paper and files can create valuable intellectual assets by utilising the data they generate as a by-product from the client work they do.

Desk research – published reports and thought leadership

We've already mentioned the importance of knowing your subject area and being familiar with what is published. On top of this, formal 'desk research' to see what has already been published is essential (if you're not familiar with the term, it means research done from your desk – such as internet searches and reading reports).

Its value is both to give you more information to help you sharpen the hypothesis, and also to avoid coming up with conclusions that are already in the public domain. It can also spark ideas you can build on.

Opinion surveys

The automatic assumption for many businesses is that thought leadership equals doing a survey of senior executives.

If you are a big global firm with lots of large clients and senior-level relationships, this is a very effective tool both for coverage and relationship maintenance (and, indeed, subtle selling). Often very big professional firms do such interviews with their own clients, but most firms are not so lucky.

For businesses without these relationships, or whose client base is a much more diverse group of SMEs, I have to warn you that utilising an agency to survey senior business people is an expensive option (senior people are hard to get hold of and don't give their time lightly), and can often bring a disappointing outcome.

Jargon-buster

Quantitative research: surveys or other structured research into large numbers of people to find out the proportion who hold different views, attitudes, knowledge or behaviour.

Qualitative research: smaller numbers of in-depth interviews or observations, where the objective is typically insight or understanding, but the findings are not statistically significant.

If you were to ask my advice (and maybe you don't want it!), if I was doing a thought leadership campaign for the first time, on a limited budget, I would strongly consider an 'omnibus survey' (see boxed section on the following page for a description of this approach) and would avoid more expensive quantitative research into difficult-to-reach audiences, unless there was a totally compelling reason.

However, if I already had a lot of clients in a particular sector, I would look to make use of them (although please note that having 'lots of SME clients' is not a defined category; you will need a more distinct group than this, eg specific sectors or those with particular characteristics, such as 'SMEs that export', 'SMEs that are family run', etc).

What are the costs and options for opinion polls by research agencies?

There are several factors that influence the cost, but the three main ones are: How many people do you want interviewed? How hard are they to reach? How many questions do you want to ask?

With specialist audiences you will need a bespoke survey, and you can quickly run up costs of £20k+ if you are doing quantitative research (ie you want a large sample to draw '20% of finance directors think X'-type conclusions).

For many firms this is prohibitively costly, and I would strongly recommend that you consider 'omnibus' surveys, which are a much cheaper alternative.

Here, they typically survey easy-to-reach groups, such as the adult population or small business owners, and you pay per question (in the region of £250 to £500).

This means you can get 10-15 questions for around £3,000. I and many others have achieved great results using low-cost omnibus surveys. If it is your first time and you do not have experienced help, I would strongly recommend them as a great starting point.

Another alternative is qualitative research. Here you have a much smaller group (say five to 10) and the interview is more in-depth. While the conclusions you draw from this won't be statistically valid, it is a great way of exploring ideas and getting the sort of depth and nuance that won't come from rigid questions. When written up in a report, it can often be highly insightful.

For qualitative research, costs start at around £4,000 for a report based on at least 10 in-depth interviews with relevant experts. If you are gauging opinions from a relatively small community, this sort of survey can be a very useful tool.

Surveys and opinion polls: getting the research right

Most people don't realise the science that goes into opinion polls and similar market research surveys.

A lot of it isn't relevant for the purposes of this book, but some of it is and we're going to go through it quickly. For a more in-depth understanding, you should get one of the many books on the subject or discuss it with the market research agency you work with.

The starting point is the size of the sample. In market research-speak the group whose opinions you want to discover is called the population, and the group you actually survey is the sample.

Cost is the biggest factor. The larger the sample, the more accurate the survey findings (and, indeed, the more credible your findings), while the larger the population, the larger the sample you need to survey for the findings to be accurate.

But it is not a linear relationship. Generally, the smaller the population, the larger the proportion of sample you need to survey.

So, for a survey of the 10 largest companies in a sector, if you survey just one or two (10-20% of the population) it won't be very representative. There is a high chance you would interview people with atypical views.

However, if you survey the UK adult population (around 48 million adults), a sample size of 2,000 (much less than 1% – in fact under 0.005%) gives a high degree of accuracy.

Why? Well there is lots of clever maths behind this, but the logic is that with large samples (of very large groups) the occasional extreme and unrepresentative answers ultimately balance out (which isn't possible in small populations unless you sample a high proportion).

Getting the questions right

Sarah Reavley of researchers Remark says: "One of the most important aspects of your research process is asking the right questions. Whether you are looking for quantitative or qualitative data, you need to be very specific about what you ask. In particular, you need to think about how you are going to analyse and respond to the data you elicit.

"Before you finalise each question ask yourself 'what information will this question produce?'. For instance, is the response something you need to support your hypothesis? Do you want 'yes/no' closed answers or expansive, descriptive responses? Can you analyse it in a useful and meaningful way? Are you looking for examples to support your argument? If so, how will you present and analyse the information your questions generate?"

So the cost and feasibility of your research will typically come down to:

- The number of interviews you need to undertake (the greater the number, the more costly the research).

- The number of questions you need to ask these people (the more questions, the more expense).

- How hard to reach the people you want to interview are (the more difficult people are to interview, the more difficult and expensive the research).

The other element that is really important is ensuring research does not have bias (all the above about sample sizes assumes that samples are representative and are surveyed 'randomly', which means there is no bias towards particular types of interviewee).

So interviews with small samples of clients, visitors to your website and email respondents suffer from this. Professional research agencies employ a lot of techniques to make sure the sample is as representative as possible (ie bias is removed).

Bias can also come from questions that are misleading or confusing (whether deliberately or inadvertently!).

Research agencies apply lots of expertise and methodologies to ensure that research is conducted rigorously.

Choosing the research agency: big name or small?

An important final factor you need to consider if using a research agency is whether you want a big name one (such as Ipsos MORI, YouGov, Gallup or the Economist Intelligence Unit) or a smaller and perhaps cheaper one.

There are pros and cons to both. A big name agency may add a bit of extra credibility, but you may also find your brand being overshadowed by the agency, with people referring to it as 'YouGov' research rather than yours!

Journalists, perhaps not surprisingly, suspect that people who give them 'do-it-yourself' surveys have not been so rigorous and are sceptical of them. They're not the only people with this view.

For instance, most UK national newspaper journalists I speak to say that they won't accept surveys with fewer than 1,000 respondents and expect them to be done by market research companies.

However, they will bend this rule if you have something credible and interesting that they really want to write about. Not long ago, the *Financial Times* ran a front-page story based on a show of hands by a few dozen practitioners at a corporate restructuring conference.

6 - Freedom of Information requests

In the UK you can request information from public bodies using a Freedom of Information (FoI) request.

Here the public body has to provide the specific bits of information you request at a nominal cost (although there are certain opt-outs they can use to avoid providing sensitive and expensive-to-gather data).

These FoI requests are great for thought leadership and PR purposes because:

- You get exclusive data at low cost.

- Its source is a government/public body (so it sounds authoritative).

- You can say something like: "This was revealed after we submitted a Freedom of Information request" which makes you sound like a campaigning sleuth revealing previously withheld data.

This technique is underused by businesses in general, but some firms have been particularly successful with it, especially some law firms active in executive immigration, and accountancy firms on tax areas.

For details of how to make a request and also for a link to lots of published examples made over recent years, go to: www.gov. uk/make-a-freedom-of-information-request/the-freedom-of-information-act. In fact, you can subscribe to get alerts to new data published in areas of interest, so you can monitor what other people are requesting.

7 - Calculations and worked examples

Examples and estimates are hugely powerful ways of conveying ideas, illustrating their impact and also grabbing the headlines.

A great example of this is each year when the UK government unveils its Budget. Among the discussions and analysis of tax changes, there will always be examples of the impact on different types of 'typical' household. These examples can be enormously strong, bringing home the impact of theoretical-sounding discussions by making them tangible and clear.

We've already talked about the importance of identifying winners and losers, and the *implications* of trends or other insights you discover. Well, to prove they are something whose effect is worth people getting bothered about, you need to put a number on it!

Big insights don't need big research programmes

Don't think that thought leadership results require huge research programmes to substantiate.

One large consultancy client had helped two big insurers to offshore large numbers of jobs to India. My client was keen to raise the profile of its expertise to get similar work in this sector and from other large businesses (at the time, offshoring call centres and similar was in its infancy in the UK).

With little more than the back of an envelope, we calculated the impact on jobs in the UK if the remaining big insurers followed suit. The estimate, over 100,000 jobs, was provided to a national journalist and ultimately resulted in more than 50 separate articles (many of them in national newspapers).

Within the first few days, the firm was approached by several large companies interested in offshoring (and also from a

---

Middle Eastern government wanting to become an offshore destination).

Were they the first company to say UK insurers were going to outsource lots overseas? No. But they were the first to put a number on it, and the first to scale it up to give a national impact – and being a large international brand, which had been involved in this already, their view had a lot of credibility with the media and their estimate was seen as authoritative.

Ten years on we revisited the estimate. Time showed that it had been pretty good and, if anything, too low (our concern at the time was that it was too high and alarmist).

CHAPTER 12

Making your findings really stand out

Talk about your findings in an interesting way

By this stage you and your team will have had plenty of great ideas, you will have narrowed these down into a hypothesis and will have investigated them – hopefully proving them, but in any case throwing up lots of insights and findings along the way, and you have explored their implications.

You will recall our definition of thought leadership:

- Original ideas
- With important implications
- Backed by evidence
- Clearly expressed
- Publicly discussed
- That strongly influence the opinions of others

Now you have to make sure that they are attention-grabbing and memorable so they can be discussed, remembered and acted upon.

Earlier in the book we case studied the huge success Gerry Boon achieved with thought leadership for Deloitte, creating its Sports Business Group in the process. He echoes this point: "It's simply not enough to have something interesting to talk about, you need to talk about it in an interesting way."

This includes defending your insights from people who would either water them down or simply turn your reports and white papers into sales documents. Peter Thomas, Accenture's UK head of marketing, warns: "You need to protect the integrity and value of your thought leadership, and you must fight salespeople and product managers. Their idea of thought leadership is a product brochure. They will invariably try to destroy its value to the reader by adding lots of stuff about services, capabilities, etc, throughout it."

Making things interesting could involve controversy, but not all subjects are controversial, nor is being provocative for the sake of it a great quality for most businesses.

Instead, let's focus on six elements. Getting these right will really help you grab the attention of your clients and others. They are:

1 – Clarity

Are your ideas expressed in simple, clear, memorable English?

People, especially big firms, often get this completely wrong and mistakenly feel that long sentences and management jargon indicate great thought leadership. It is quite the reverse. Think about people who are great communicators – they don't exhort people with phrases such as 'leverage your core competencies'.

For every important idea in your thought leadership, concentrate hard at explaining it in crystal-clear English.

Big ideas… not big words

A while ago I was helping a management consultant in a large firm with his article for publication in a magazine, and it was full of jargon. You can imagine… lots of guff like 'leverage core competencies', 'focus on key drivers' and 'implement global best practices'.

I took a fair amount of time to understand what he was saying and rewrote it so it was expressed in clear English. The ideas that emerged seemed pretty common sense and nothing exceptional.

I asked him if I had understood him correctly. Yes, indeed I had understood him correctly, but he wanted the article in the jargon because he felt it wasn't very impressive when explained in clear English.

I am not denying there may well be a market in which consultants from big firms pitch up, give a load of management BS and some people buy it! Nonetheless, if you find your ideas look simplistic and trite when expressed in clear English, the reality is that they probably are.

If you are going to be influential you need to sort out some better insights, rather than dress up weak ones in jargon.

2 – Have interesting numbers

The key word here is 'interesting'.

There are lots of reports stuffed full of dull numbers. You need to pull out the small number of statistics that vividly illustrate your point.

If you have lots of numbers, that's great – stick them in an appendix at the back.

Concentrate on the small number of really important and memorable numbers your research has unearthed — and if it hasn't, find some!

Why numbers are really important to making you a thought leader

Numbers imply science

People are simultaneously able to hold contradictory viewpoints without realising it. Statistics are a great example of this.

On the one hand we all know the expression 'lies, damned lies and statistics' — it is an expression that you may have used yourself. Yet when a number is attached to something it nonetheless gives it a seemingly scientific legitimacy that makes people pay it far more attention and respect.

Economics is the ultimate example of this: lots of numbers, lots of data, lots of confident predictions. However, ultimately every calculation is based on a lot of assumptions.

Nonetheless, creating a number implies a rigorous and scientific process.

Numbers are memorable

OK, most numbers are not memorable but some of them are. Advertisers know this, which is why everyone knows that eight out of 10 cats prefer Whiskas.

After all, which of the following slogans works best: 'Nearly all cats prefer Whiskas'; 'The vast majority of cats prefer Whiskas'; 'Eight out of 10 cats prefer Whiskas'?

This is, of course, why politicians love to bandy about statistics too. They know having a number on something is both memorable and credible.

Numbers give impact

How many is 'a lot of jobs' or how much is 'a large amount of money'? Such terms are relative and subjective, which is why they are weak.

"Closing the factory will result in a lot of job losses" is less memorable and specific than saying: "Closing the factory will cause the loss of 2,000 jobs directly and many more at its suppliers." Better still: "Closing the factory will cost well over 4,000 jobs – 2,000 employees and an estimated 2,000 at suppliers."

Having numbers is really, really important for press coverage

Perhaps the audience that over-attaches the most validity to numbers is the media.

Assuming you don't want your thought leadership to be a 'best kept secret' and that you're looking to use it to build up a very valuable reputation, you're going to be looking to get press coverage.

So make sure you have numbers that illustrate the important points you are making and, specifically, illustrate their impact on readers of the publication.

3 – Highlight the implications

We've already highlighted in earlier chapters the need to identify, discuss and illustrate the implications of your insights. It is going to be the implications of your findings that are the interesting bits – explore them, and also the implications of the implications!

But don't talk about them in vague terms like 'a lot of people will be worse off'. Be specific. Which groups, by how much and what will be the impact on them? Who will end up as the winners and the losers?

4 – Colourful stories, analogies and metaphors

The best communicators use colourful stories and metaphors to make their ideas clear and memorable.

By way of an example, Damian McKinney, one of my clients, runs a successful international management consultancy that he co-founded 15 years ago. He is a natural communicator and always uses clear and succinct analogies when describing things, often drawing on his former career in the Royal Marines.

When he describes the difference between 'strategy' and 'vision' to clients and journalists, he doesn't jump into a business school definition. Instead he uses plain English and a vivid analogy: "Your vision is what you want to achieve and your strategy is how you'll do it. An example from the military would be that your vision is to take the hill so you can win the battle; the strategy is to do it at night, when the enemy is asleep."

He also has plenty of colourful stories that illustrate his approach – whether from business projects or his military past. It goes down great with journalists and his clients.

But this is something anyone can do… if they take the time to prepare properly. Make sure you have memorable analogies and stories to add impact to your ideas.

5– Think visually

A picture paints a thousand words, and as you may not have the attention of your reader for that long you need to think visually about how to reinforce your points.

Charts, infographics, short videos, Mind Maps, photographs and other visual tools are important to convey your ideas to all readers and are particularly important for the 'visual thinkers' among your audience.

Florence Nightingale and the importance of visual images

Florence Nightingale is best known for her role in the Crimean War and her nursing that saved many, many soldiers from the biggest killer – not their Russian enemy, but the poor care and insanitary conditions of military 'hospitals'.

When she returned to London she campaigned for improvements and backed up her arguments with data in tables on the massive numbers of preventable deaths.

She found that these had surprisingly little impact, so she became an early innovator in the graphical representation of data, vividly illustrating her case with the use of such then innovative techniques as the polar area diagram (a form of pie chart). She subsequently became the first female member of the Royal Statistical Society.

If it was necessary for Florence Nightingale to resort to vivid graphics to make her point on a literally 'life and death' matter in an age with little media and few distractions, it certainly is necessary for your reports now we are in an age with many media and constant distractions!

6 – Practicality

The importance of your thought leadership having practical applications for the people you are targeting was something that came across strongly from the people I interviewed for this book. The last thing you want is for people to read your ideas and think *That's a really important issue but what on earth can I do?*

Robert Pay, business development director at international management consultants Alvarez & Marsal says: "The best thought leadership has practical and useful elements. A good example is law firm Taylor Wessing's Global Intellectual Property Index, now in its sixth year. It answered a real need to get comparative views on the relative attractiveness of jurisdictions. Interestingly, some of the countries which scored poorly have started to get serious about reforming their IP laws. It also gave the firm a leg-up in debates about IP issues."

Whatever your conclusions and insights, make sure there is something practical that can be done as a result. For instance, highlight what people should do to take advantage of the opportunity you have identified or protect themselves against the problem you are warning them about.

Quality talks… and the importance of a thorough peer review

The other element that makes your thought leadership stand out is the quality.

Obvious, but there are lots of firms issuing poor-quality thought leadership, thinking it's great. How do you make sure you are not one of them?

Clearly, if you've followed the process in this book you have done everything humanly possible, and you have already had a modest peer review by discussing your hypothesis with colleagues and clients.

What you want to do is have a strong peer review on your findings and content before it goes out of the door.

At Accenture the quality check comes from a rigorous peer review. It is assessed against eight dimensions with specific measures (eg relevance to the intended audience) and reviewers score it. If scores aren't strong it has to be improved before going any further.

> ## The importance of quality (and maintaining it)
>
> Terry Corby is a strategy and marketing consultant who has seen thought leadership at the highest levels, not least through having previously been the Global Head of Thought Leadership Marketing at Accenture and a Partner and the Chief Marketing & Communications officer at KPMG.
>
> He is emphatic that businesses of all sizes need to maintain the quality of their material.
>
> He highlights the example of one firm he advised, and says: "This firm did a lot of thought leadership, but the quality was highly variable. In their core area of expertise they did a lot of reports that were really good, and they did have a few nuggets on other subjects too.
>
> "But there was no process and rigour, so the quality of output was too variable. As an example, it also issued lots of research based on small samples, often in areas where the firm really didn't have deep enough expertise to give much insight. This meant the good output got lost among the dross – when you went into its offices there were literally racks of reports.
>
> "The problem with this was really brought home when I visited some of their clients. One senior director told me how he was so fed up with poor-quality material from the firm that he had ordered his PA to intercept and bin anything they sent without him even seeing it!"

You should do the same.

The Bloom Group (www.bloomgroup.com) is a great thought leadership agency in the US that publishes all sorts of interesting and useful material about thought leadership.

They talk about seven factors to test to ensure that your thought leadership will have impact. I borrowed heavily from their list in recommending you to get your reviewers to assess your thought leadership on at least the following criteria:

1. Clarity – are your ideas clearly and memorably expressed?

2. Relevance – do the findings have strong relevance to your audience and their needs?

3. Novelty – are your findings and recommendations new and distinctive?

4. Validity – is there sufficient proof for your conclusions and recommendations?

5. Rigour – is your analysis and its explanation consistent and logical?

6. Impact – is the impact on companies and/or their stakeholders clear in the report?

7. Practicality – can your target audience actually take action as a result of your recommendations?

A template peer assessment sheet for you to adapt and use is below. It is available to download from www.kelsopr.com/thought-leadership-manual-resources

Template assessment form for peer reviews

The intended audience for this report is: (add description of target audience here)					
	Not at all	A bit	Strong	Very strong	Comments
Are the ideas clearly and memorably expressed?					
Do the findings have strong relevance to the intended audience and their needs?					
Are the findings and recommendations new and distinctive?					
Is there sufficient proof for the conclusions and recommendations?					
Is the analysis and its explanation consistent and logical?					
Is the impact on companies and/or their stakeholders clear in the report?					
Can the target audience take action as a result of the recommendations?					
Will the report be of interest to your relevant clients and prospects?					

Should your thought leadership be provocative?

Several of the people I spoke to while writing this book also felt that it was important for thought leadership to be provocative – not necessarily meaning that it would provoke people, but certainly that it would be thought provoking and challenge established viewpoints.

It is great if your thought leadership is thought provoking, and often this is essential if you are going to stand out. People who work with me know that I often push for initiatives to challenge existing viewpoints as strongly as possible.

But it isn't always needed. A great example is on page 179 in Chapter 13, where Clifford Chance made a big impact and stole a march on their rivals simply by providing timely and practical advice at a time of great uncertainty in the financial markets. It worked through being clear and practical, not thought provoking – which was the last thing its recipients needed at the time!

CHAPTER 13

Thought leadership on a limited budget

This book has deliberately steered clear of using illustrations that require lots of money or some sort of exclusive access.

Even the examples from large firms have involved limited cost initiatives because I have wanted to emphasise that thought leadership is not something for big firms with large budgets, it is something for all organisations, even one-man bands.

If you are investing a lot in such initiatives, you should still apply the methodology in this book rigorously, regardless of the budget being used (perhaps more so given the need to generate even stronger results to get a good ROI when budgets are large). However, the approach in this book works really well for firms with few resources (except good professional expertise and a desire to succeed!).

The most important area to focus on is exploiting whatever thought leadership you create, so make sure you have the time and resources to do this. You will get much more business, for example, from a case study that is well exploited than from a big survey and report that you don't support.

Ideas for getting a big bang with limited buck

If you have a very limited budget, some great and inexpensive ways of getting ideas, insights, evidence and content for a campaign include:

- Hosting discussions, dinners and round tables

- Case studies

- In-depth qualitative interviews

- Analysis of public data and information

- Analysis of own data

- Calculations and extrapolations from experience

- Freedom of Information requests

- Projects with industry associations

- Omnibus surveys

If you do just one thing, host a dinner!

If you are going to do just one thing, I would strongly advise holding a dinner and inviting a few lively clients and prospects along to talk about a common issue. Think about having someone chair the discussion or be a speaker, but it isn't essential.

When large companies spend millions on television advertising campaigns, the first thing they do is have a focus group in which members of the public talk about the issue and the product.

A client discussion dinner is your focus group! Lots of ideas will flow – keep a subtle note, as this will provide a great starting point for your thought leadership.

I have to say it often takes a lot of persuasion to get some firms to do one of these (they are often scared it might expose their lack of knowledge on the issue). Don't have such worries!

Afterwards they have always said how useful it was and how they must do more; often the very act of getting together with clients generates a project as a bonus.

It's great ideas, not great budgets, that matter

Former Touche Ross (now Deloitte) partner Gerry Boon (case studied in Chapter 1 for his hugely successful thought leadership initiative that created its Sports Business Group), says: "The best thought leadership is often a very simple, straightforward perspective. The planning, research and compilation to execute the process may be detailed, but the idea itself will often be compelling in its simplicity."

At leading international law firm Clifford Chance there are resources and an internal support team for grand projects, but even there the best initiatives often simply come from a good idea executed at the right time with minimal costs.

A great example was the firm's response to the Eurozone crisis. While other firms were producing documents, often lengthy, that went into great detail on the legal background to the Euro departure options, Clifford Chance took a different and more practical approach.

Where it distinguished itself was by focusing on an audience that was concerned less with the theory and more on the practicalities: those in banks on the frontline managing transactions and grappling with how to deal with them amid the turmoil and uncertainty.

Banking partner Kate Gibbons, who also has responsibility for overseeing the firm's thought leadership, says: "We framed these briefings in a format which posed practical questions and sought to answer them briefly over a couple of pages. They were repurposed across a number of different product groups, always using the same basic structure.

"They were a big success. Clients treated these briefings as a manual during the financial turmoil, and we received exceptionally good feedback. Many clients asked us to come and present on the subject, and it led to requests to provide advice too.

"Besides distributing them to our clients, the briefings were also posted on the websites of various influential and cross-border trade associations, so leading to additional wide exposure.

"It was a particularly successful initiative which really revolved around providing advice in a practical manner, at a time of great need for clarity, given the uncertainty these exceptional events were causing in the financial markets."

Steve Blundell of professional firm strategy consultancy Redstone Consultants also has a great example of a low-cost initiative working really well (very much to his surprise). He explains: "I did a survey using a paper insert in a client's newsletter. It received 27 responses, which I wrote up as a small thought piece as the results, around the subject of innovation, were quite unusual.

"To my surprise it got coverage a few days later in the *Financial Times* and, consequently, I was asked to speak at a conference in Nice as a result of my 'expertise'!"

SECTION IV
GRABBING THE ATTENTION OF CLIENTS AND THE MARKET

Chapter 14 - Getting your content right

Chapter 15 - Making your marketing work

Chapter 16 - Getting in the world's top media

CHAPTER 14

Getting your content right

We will be looking at getting the content right in this section.

Having thought about your target audiences and their requirements, you need to have content that will present your findings in the best way to get their engagement.

After all, you want them to look at your findings, understand them and remember them. You also want them to be impressed and change their opinion and behaviours as a result, including feeling even more positive towards your business.

By getting the content 'right', I don't mean that I will be giving lots of advice on producing pretty reports and laying out your press release correctly.

As important as these are, there is plenty of advice on such things already online and in books, and I really don't think the sum total of human happiness is going to be increased by me adding yet more to this mountain of information. If you would like this sort of granular advice, please see www.kelsopr.com/thought-leadership-manual-resources where I have added recommendations for books and online guides.

Instead, what we'll be doing is helping you choose what is right for *your* campaign. For instance, should you write a blog, a white paper or a book? Something else perhaps?

Does it have to be a report or can parts be presented compellingly as podcasts or video, for instance? Is one report the right approach or is breaking it into a series of initiatives better?

Content re-thought for busy people on the move

Peter Thomas, Accenture's UK head of marketing says: "People need to think carefully about the channel so the content is in a form your prospects will engage with.

"We don't email big clunky PDFs any longer, for instance. Instead we are taking different approaches, such as our mobile-optimised site Click-Accenture, where our ideas are presented as articles with no more than 250 words so they are suitable for people with little time."

If everyone else is emailing PDFs, a video or something presented live is so much more memorable.

To help you decide, on the following pages is a short checklist of some of the things you might consider, together with their pros and cons, with some of them considered in more detail afterwards.

Even big firms don't have the resources to do everything, so you need to focus on the things that will work well with your targets.

However, I strongly urge you to use this as an opportunity to experiment. If all your competitors are sending white papers and you create a podcast or video, it is you that stands out as different.

Choosing the right form for your content is key to having the best possible impact with your targets.

Thought leadership: what content is right for your audiences?

Type of content	Pros	Cons	How to make them work well
Report A longish document (say 10-40+ pages) outlining your findings, research, etc	Good for those audiences who want to see the detail. Shows thoroughness and depth.	It can take a lot of time. Often there is a temptation to put in padding. Can be costly to produce and print.	Have an 'executive summary' document for most readers, with the full report for select audiences (maybe at a charge to some, such as non clients).
White paper Part report, part article, this document sets out a viewpoint or analysis on a particular theme	Can be produced quickly and cheaply with a minimum of fuss.	None if done well – they're one of the best ways of showing your expertise (although if written badly they can be dry and overly technical).	Ensure it is thought-provoking and interesting, not a glorified brochure. Ensure clear 'calls to action' to develop the relationship further.
Article A 500 to, say, 2,000+ word viewpoint or analysis	Can be produced quickly and cheaply with a minimum of fuss. Can be published in the media, and reused in a blog and all sorts of places.	None if done well (although if written badly can be dry and technical or, worse, vague and generic).	Ensure it is thought-provoking and interesting.
Case study	Highly credible way of showing expertise. One of the most versatile and persuasive forms of marketing content. Quick and cheap to produce (in theory).	Some organisations make heavy weather of asking clients. Some clients don't want their name to be used – all adding up to a long and protracted process.	Start early (to allow time for political delays). Ensure it is thought-provoking and interesting (not a glossed-over version). Can be stand-alone or in report/video.
Blog	A quick way of publishing regular ideas and comments online – attracting followers and boosting your rankings on Google.	One blog post by itself looks odd and won't have much impact... you have to do them regularly.	Before you start, create an editorial schedule for the next few months to show you can sustain it with ideas and content.

Thought leadership: what content is right for your audiences? (CONTINUED)

Type of content	Pros	Cons	How to make them work well
Book	Nothing establishes an expert like a book. Writing involves creating a huge amount of content that you can reuse.	Takes a lot of time and effort.	Reuse the material you produce for the book elsewhere. Get advice from specialists in producing business books. It's not about book sales, it's about sales of *your services* the book promotes.
Video For your website and YouTube	Shows you in action (capturing your personality). Can bring in graphics, animation and interviews to clarify complex points. Delivers emotion as well as facts.	Can be expensive if it needs sophisticated production. Some people just don't come across well on video.	Think carefully about your audience and your message. Is video suitable, and can you do it well and within budget? Practice *a lot* before presenting.
Podcast An audio recording for downloading from the internet	Conveys your personality and passion. You can 'do it yourself' at low cost. Huge potential audience on iTunes.	None if done well – they are very powerful. Bad if you drone on in a monotone.	Research how to make a successful podcast. Invest in good microphones. Don't read a script. Need to promote it effectively.
Infographic An eyecatching image to present data on a webpage	Can go viral and get lots of views. Can present complex data compellingly.	None if done well.	Make it interesting and memorable. Promote it. Keep it simple! Reuse it in your other marketing.
Speech	People see you in action. You have everyone's attention for 30 minutes.	You are limited by audience size. If you deliver it only once, the preparation time is high	Reuse the content (eg present it several times, turn it into a podcast, video, article, SlideShare, etc). Don't just turn up and deliver. Make the most of the event for networking and prospecting.
Personal presentation Get out and meet your clients etc	'People buy people' – you have got to get out and meet them if they are going to buy or recommend you.	Time-consuming if you meet the 'wrong' people (or if you waste the time of the 'right' people).	Research and prepare ahead of each meeting. Get someone to book meetings for you. Adapt the material to the business. Don't present – listen and discuss.

Make sure your content works in a mobile world

According to Ofcom (the regulator for the communications industries) as of the first quarter of 2014, 57% of adults used mobile handsets to access the internet (up from 49% a year earlier).

No doubt, by the time you are reading this it will be higher through the spread of 4G and even greater ownership of lightweight tablets, iPads, and whatever else comes along.

All of this has implications for your content as many people have changed the way they consume information, particularly while they are on the move. This includes:

- You need to think of what content will work best on mobiles. Information needs to be punchier and visual, while there are now options for some degree of interactivity.

- Think about video and particularly podcasts. After all, people like to listen to things when walking, driving and commuting.

- If you are emailing people with links to your website, you need one that works well on mobile platforms – whether smaller smartphones or bigger tablets.

- Many firms have created apps to distribute their thought leadership. It is well worth considering, but don't do it just because others have; think about whether it is something your clients and others actually use.

Writing a business book – what are the options?

I'd particularly like to go through in more detail one of the options from the previous chart: creating your own book.

While it might sound a big undertaking, there's nothing that positions you better as an expert than having a book.

Not only does it give you huge bragging rights, it helps in all sorts of other ways. Some of these include:

- People who buy and read it will contact you (and you will reach a potentially huge audience by making it available through Amazon and, if it's good, bookshops and airport newsagents).

- You are much more attractive as a speaker for event organisers.

- It is a great handout for prospects you meet and for targeted mailings to your top targets.

- You can reuse the content in all sorts of ways to create blogs, white papers, podcasts and webinars with little extra effort.

For many people it is not the right option, but it could be for those with a great theme, plenty of determination and who are willing to set aside the time.

Writing a book is a big undertaking (as I found out!), but it may not be as big a project as many people think. There are certain short cuts, although even with these to go from start to finish in under a year is pretty fast.

Instead, many people start a book and get stuck. It could be because they have difficulty finding the time or with the writing process, causing them to lose momentum and give up.

Often, people fall into the trap of permanently rewriting the first chapter as their ideas change.

I have summarised the options in the chart below on page 190. Most people are well aware of book publishers who will take your manuscript, create a book and pay you royalties from the sales. Most people are also aware you can self-publish.

In creating this book, I took the middle option – assisted publishing. With this I paid a fee and got lots of great coaching and support from The Book Midwife. Most of my clients who've gone down the book route have used a similar option, whether with the Book Midwife, LID Publishing or other companies in this market.

For most business and professional people this is the best option (except those writing bestsellers or those in very technical areas such as law, tax, etc, where there are specialist publishers).

This is because for you, as someone on the launch pad of becoming a thought leader, the purpose of writing a book is not to make lots of money through its sales. The sad reality is most business books only sell a few thousand copies – not enough to cover the time involved, let alone for you to give up your day job.

Their benefit comes from positioning you strongly as an expert, allowing you to win more work, more easily at a higher chargeable rate.

Being an author also opens doors to interviews, while if you want to get on the conference speaking circuit, being an author of a book puts you head and shoulders above everyone else (or at least everyone without a book) and is something that speaker bookers particularly look for.

The fee for this option is in the £5k-£10k region. For some people this will be a lot of money, but to professionals reading this book it should be put into the context of how much time it will save them compared to doing it themselves (or having to market themselves to lots of publishers) and how much time it will save by giving them proper support to get the book done.

Quite frankly, it isn't a huge amount when you compare it to the cost of, say, creating a brochure or what people pay for their season ticket for the pleasure of commuting into London!

Options for becoming a business author

	Self-publish	Assisted publishing (co-operative publishing)	Commercial book publisher
What is it?	You write the book yourself and pay a book publisher to create it.	The publisher makes much of their money by helping you create a book (for which they charge a fee). They will support you with professional know-how and a team, and help bring it to the attention of book stores (online and high street).	Mainstream book publishers make their money through sales of books (with no upfront fee payable by the author).
Pros	Cheap (if you have already written a book and simply want it published).	Will help coach you through the whole process. Will have a professional team looking after all the stuff in the background – ensuring it looks great, is properly sub-edited and proofread, and distributed to book stores. In short, you benefit from their know-how. Will work with books likely to have niche audiences.	Great for themes where there will be a large market. If a book has strong potential they can put their muscle behind it.
Cons	You have to do everything yourself (or at least you have to organise everything yourself). The only person providing quality control is you (which isn't great, given that you will be strongly emotionally attached to the book but not terribly experienced).	Bit of a cottage industry at present, so don't expect the business to be operating 'at industrial scale'. You pay a fee of typically £5-£10k.	As a new author you are a small cog in a big wheel. Only interested in books that are going to sell well (many business books are pretty niche and won't be of interest). You may have to spend an awful lot of effort marketing your idea to different publishers to get a taker.

CHAPTER 15

Making your marketing work

In the previous chapter, we talked about the importance of getting the content right. Sadly, no matter how brilliant your content is, you need to publicise and distribute it to the right people – whether clients, prospects, referrers, opinion formers or whoever it is you're looking to reach.

This is the point at which you start having to make tactical marketing decisions: should you email, seek press coverage, form alliances, speak at events or have a brilliant web page, for example? In marketing-speak, these different ways of delivering your message (and sales) are channels.

On the one hand, a combination of channels is invariably necessary. On the other hand, the more activities you undertake, the more time and resources are required. At some point, you will spread yourself too thinly, so focus achieves better results than pursuing every opportunity.

There are hundreds of books on how to do PR effectively, thousands on advertising and a whole industry has sprung up publishing advice on using social media effectively.

> **Marketing 'how to do its'**
>
> There isn't room, nor is it desirable, for me to turn this book into a tutorial on every type of marketing. If you aren't experienced in a particular type of marketing activity and want to know more, there are lots of good books and plenty of online advice. I have highlighted a few at www.kelsopr.com/thought-leadership-manual-resources

What I can do is give a few pros and cons for things that work well in the context of thought leadership.

> Experienced firms tend to put most of their efforts into ensuring the maximum use of their thought leadership with existing clients, contacts and referrers. Your biggest focus should be on this too.

For instance, firms new to thought leadership often put all their energy into targeting 'the market' with publicity, conference sponsorships and direct marketing.

There is nothing wrong with this, but it is worth noting that more experienced firms tend to put most of their efforts elsewhere (and tend to see this activity as important but not critical). Their biggest focus is on ensuring the maximum use is made by their partners or sales teams with existing clients, contacts and referrers. Your biggest focus should be on them too.

For instance:

- Other people in your firm, especially those in sales or with client relationships: how are you going to communicate it to them and engage them in using it to create meetings and sales with 'their' clients? Are you going to meet with them, present to them, provide them with template information and/or identify specific clients where the subject is particularly applicable? Will they have targets for generating meetings and sales?

- Your firm will have people who are great referrers. Do you know who they are and, if so, what focus will you put on meeting, briefing and schmoozing them so they can work their magic in this area? And what about great contacts who aren't referrers but should be – where do they fit in your priority?

- Lapsed clients and unsuccessful tenders are also fruitful. They know you and may simply be waiting for you to get back in touch. They are a whole lot easier to sell to than people you've never met before. Put them on the list and give 'em a call!

- Your firm's alumni (former employees who have left). These people know the firm well and usually have fond memories of their time and former colleagues. They are often great referrers, and many will have moved into roles that make them either good prospects or able to introduce you. If your firm has an alumni programme, tap into this (and if it doesn't, track them down on LinkedIn).

- Brainstorm other types of people who know you and your firm well whom you can enlist subtly into becoming part of your enlarged network of referrers.

Marketing while you are asleep

Some aspects of marketing and sales are pretty time-consuming. Writing articles, making presentations, going to breakfast networking events all take lots of time and once they are done, well, they are done and gone.

Wouldn't it be good to have some form of marketing that doesn't involve continual effort on your part? Something you could set up and it would regularly bring in leads for months and months without much additional effort on your part, even while you are asleep.

In fact, there is such a way, and using your thought leadership insights to produce interesting content helps make it work particularly successfully.

In the first section we talked about how buyers, including executives and business owners, are increasingly searching online for solutions to their problems. I am sure you do it too.

In a nutshell, the term 'inbound marketing' has arisen to describe how you take advantage of all this searching on Google.

It is not just a question of appearing prominently on Google, although that is an important element. Nor is it a question of having your phone number and 'contact us' box prominent; as most people are in searching mode, not buying mode, they won't get in touch.

It is all about having something tempting that the person will want to have (and in the process provide you with their email address) – this is called a 'lead magnet'. And once you have their email this enables you to send further documents and invitations, moving them closer and closer to becoming a client.

This is where your thought leadership comes in since it enables you to create a powerful lead magnet and other content for a great inbound marketing programme.

For more about this, see the guide on www.kelsopr.com/thought-leadership-manual-resources

Using your thought leadership to make 'inbound marketing' work

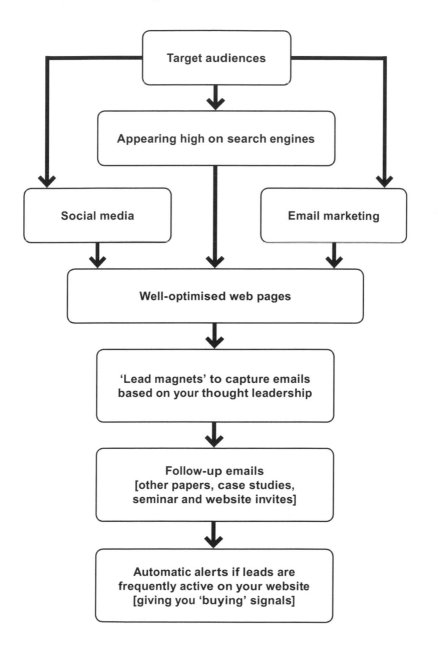

Getting to the top of Google

Google is the pre-eminent search engine and I typically find that about 90% of search traffic to the websites I monitor comes via Google, compared to other search engines such as Bing (its nearest rival) and Yahoo.

Being at the top of Google when people search for help in the areas where you are an expert is a very powerful place. It is the difference between having a shop window on London's Oxford Street or in a sleepy country town. Many B2B firms are in the latter.

You can check whether this is the same for your website by looking at your visitor data (if you don't know how to do this, ask the company website manager for it).

Its importance in the context of your thought leadership and using it as a 'lead magnet' is that the process requires regular traffic to your website, which typically requires you appearing prominently on Google when people search (or an awful lot of activity on social media!).

Search Engine Optimisation (SEO) – what does it mean?

SEO is the jargon term for getting your website to the top of Google when people make relevant searches for your goods or services. It is, broadly, making various adjustments to the text and other elements of your webpages to attract Google and other search engines. There are other techniques, such as also having lots of links to your page on social media and from other websites.

If you appear prominently at the top of Google you will get a lot of visits to your website from potential clients. You get fewer visitors the lower you are on page 1 of the search results and it falls off even more dramatically if you are on page 2 or below.

If you want to come top for a high-frequency search term such as 'insurance' or 'holiday' then you will almost certainly need to use a specialist and spend a lot of time and money.

However, for most professional and business-to-business companies this isn't the case. With a bit of thought and planning and, of course, activity and monitoring, you can get on to the front page of Google quite easily for many of the likely searches that matter to you.

> For most professional and business-to-business firms a bit of thought and planning can get you on to the front page of Google quite easily for the likely searches that matter to you.

Why is this? It is because:

- Most professional and B2B firms are surprisingly rubbish at search engine optimisation and many have a phobia of using Google AdWords (the other way of getting to the top of Google).

- People looking for your services will often put in something quite specific, such as 'Tax specialist North London' or 'Employment Lawyer Glasgow' or 'BPR tips for manufacturers'.

These specific searches are often called 'long tail searches' because they contain three or four key words. While there are a lot fewer of these specific searches, the people doing them have something specific on their mind and are likely prospects.

Being at the top of Google is one of the most powerful places for your business to be; it is the equivalent of having a shop front at Oxford Circus or in Bond Street.

Conference speaking, direct marketing and networking are all important, but they are also transitory unless you keep doing them.

If you get to the top of Google for these long tail search phrases, it's often relatively easy and low maintenance to stay up there, yet your marketing is working 24/7 for you, continually grabbing the attention of anyone using these searches. For more on getting your practice to the top of Google, go to www.kelsopr.com/thought-leadership-manual-resources

Social media and thought leadership

I thought long and hard about including a section on using social media effectively. On the one hand, it is easy to be cynical in a business-to-business context about Twitter and LinkedIn forums.

On the other hand, it is really important and those people who invest the time to develop know-how on how to get the best out of it do get good results.

So sharing thoughts and tips is important, but a book has a long shelf life, while social media is changing all the time.

It's a conundrum! So rather than include a section that will almost certainly be out of date by the time you read it, I am going to cover this online in an area exclusively for readers, so it can be kept up to date.

For up-to-date advice on using social media to add impact and reach to your thought leadership (and your marketing), please go to: www.kelsopr.com/thought-leadership-manual-resources

CHAPTER 16

Getting in the world's top media

OK – I'm a PR person by background so there has to be some PR stuff in the book.

There is tons of stuff online about writing press releases, doing great articles and preparing for TV interviews. If you need this help, please see the resources on www.kelsopr.com/thought-leadership-manual-resources

Instead, let's cut to the chase. You want to be in the *Financial Times* and *The Economist*, not *Widget Monthly*, don't you? Great, here's how to do it…

How to get in the *Financial Times*

For many business people, getting their thought leadership into the *Financial Times* is the be-all-and-end-all.

Being quoted there brings strong credibility, makes sure you are noticed by hard-to-reach senior audiences, often directly brings client leads and also confers on you huge "as I said the other week in the *FT*" bragging rights.

As such, journalists on the *Financial Times* are spoilt for choice, with people offering them their comments and thought leadership. So if you want to get into it, you and your PR adviser (if you have one – if not, speak to me!) are going to have to do your homework.

Nonetheless, the *Financial Times* has more pages dedicated to business than just about all the other UK daily national newspapers put together. So if you produce something of quality that is strongly relevant to its readership, and then play the PR game the right way, there's a good chance of getting in.

As with any publication, if you want to get into it the first thing you will have to do is buy copies and scrutinise them, and its website.

Questions you should ask yourself are:

- **Who are the people it is writing for?** In the case of the *FT* this includes people working in the City (banks and other financial institutions, professions, regulators) and those in the financial markets more generally around the rest of the world; investors generally, especially those interested in technology; senior business leaders (and those who want to be one); and the global business elite more generally. Its weekend edition also has a lot of wealthy lifestyle features that attract people who don't read it during the week.

- **What are the sorts of story it likes to report?**

- **What are the newspaper's and website's different sections, and where would my thought leadership fit in?**

- **Which journalists write on the subjects relevant to me, and what tends to interest them?**

- **What elements go into prominent thought leadership-led stories?**

- **Has the *FT* covered this story before? What angles did it take and what elements did the article contain?**

If being in the *FT* is your goal, design your thought leadership to contain the sorts of angles and elements it wants to include in its articles.

The next stage is dealing with the journalists once your thought leadership is ready.

Most journalists are short-term, in-a-rush sorts of people who fulfil vital roles in the ultimate just-in-time production process. They typically have hectic days and expect people to queue up to see them (they don't queue up to see you!) and operate to their rules.

This applies just as much to the *Financial Times*, although it is worth noting that its recent 2014 redesign involves a switch to longer articles, which are research led. Not only does it seem to be forcing its journalists to plan more articles in advance, it is also creating more opportunity for prominent articles for stories with strong supporting data – such as your thought leadership.

The best results come from you approaching journalists, whether on the *FT* or elsewhere, with plenty of patience and flexibility; don't expect them to fit in with your rigid launch plans or drop everything because you want them to.

The following charts summarise some of the best ways to get into the *Financial Times*.

How to get into the Financial Times

Section	What it covers	Tips on how to do it
The News, Companies and Markets sections	Be clear that the newspaper has different sections, each with different journalists writing for them, and different requirements. Think of them as separate departments with big barriers – even though they sit in an open plan office a few yards from each other! For instance, UK news stories go in the UK News pages and international news goes on the International pages (Duh!). Trading, commodity and financial market stories typically go in the second section, as do most listed company announcements. However, if something is really interesting, it will get hauled up to the main news pages towards the front. There is a lot more to it than I can cover here, so buy the newspaper and study the website and you'll start to see what goes where and when.	To get into these sections, study which journalists tend to write on the subject relevant to you. Approach them with the offer of an 'exclusive' (which actually means they will get it ahead of everybody else, not exclusively for all time). The more leeway in terms of timing you give them, the more likely you are to be successful. Often journalists like to run thought leadership stories on Mondays because the weekend is a quiet time for news (which means they write them up a few days before Sunday). Use this to your advantage.
Letters to the Editor	Virtually all publications have a Letters to the Editor section, and it is a much underused way of getting coverage, despite being a well-read part of the paper – for instance, whenever I have had a letter published, I've always had lots of emails from my contacts, saying they've read it.	Follow this formula: Write a short, punchy letter with the first paragraph referencing an article that has appeared in the paper within the past two or three days. The remaining two or three paragraphs (no more) should either rebut it, highlight a quirky aspect, share an amusing anecdote, or elaborate on a point that's particularly important. Send it to letters.editor@FT.com (do it yourself – not via your PR or marketing advisor) at about 10am. Include a contact phone number. Using this formula gives me and my clients a 75% strike rate (ie three out of four get printed).

How to get into the Financial Times (CONTINUED)

Section	What it covers	Tips on how to do it
Reports / Supplements	The *Financial Times* regularly contains a whole range of extra reports on subjects ranging from specific countries (for instance, a must-read on 'Doing business in Wallonia' is scheduled as I write!) to Energy, Private Banking and The Future of the Car. The full list is available via **www.ft.com/special-reports**	Synopses of what is planned for these sections are usually prepared and issued a few weeks in advance. Study them and select a couple of sections (no more) to which you can bring something distinctive. The synopses often advise you to send your ideas to the supplement's editorial email. Do this, but don't hold your breath! For the best chance of appearing, work out well in advance which journalists are likely to contribute and approach them directly (bearing in mind that they will probably not be named in the synopses).
Regular sections	The *Financial Times* has certain sections that appear weekly or monthly. At the moment, these include: ◆ FTFM (its Monday supplement for the fund management industry). ◆ Executive Appointments (its Thursday supplement combining career advice and related articles with senior job ads). ◆ Connected Business (its monthly supplement about business and technology). ◆ Various columns, some quirky, that appear weekly in its features section – such as its Working Smarter column.	While I could write a chapter about getting into each, the general advice is to get to know each supplement and the sorts of ideas it likes. Then approach the editor of the section with something really appropriate and distinctive. Be really flexible on the timing and don't expect them to jump to include it in the very next edition. Target the journalists (some of them staff, some of them freelance), who contribute regularly – they are usually on the lookout for ideas for their columns. Connected Business typically posts a synopsis of its forthcoming features, available via **www.ft.com/special-reports**

How to get into *The Economist*

I often get requests to get spokespeople into *The Economist* magazine, although many seem to come from people who don't read it!

There are first of all a few things to bear in mind about *The Economist*:

- It isn't a newspaper as such; it is a weekly magazine based on comment and analysis. It is not at all interested in exclusives around your recent research in the way that daily newspapers are.

- *The Economist* writers typically interview several people for the analysis articles they write, and many of them don't get quoted. Similarly, because it is comment, not news reporting, articles typically get put in the authoritative voice of *The Economist*, meaning the writer may well take your views and attribute them to the magazine or simply put something like "industry leaders think..."

- While it has a UK section, it is firmly an international publication, so what you are offering needs to have resonance with the global business elite.

Assuming your business is not the sort that 'hobnobs' at Davos each year, here is how to get in:

- Study the publication and website thoroughly!

- *The Economist* never carries articles from outside authors, so if your plan is to get an article written by you in it, forget it! However, it does attribute people who appear in the Letters to Editor section, so this is a good alternative option to consider.

- *The Economist* magazine (not so the website), never attributes articles to particular journalists. Luckily it has an online directory listing the journalists and their particular interests. Quite frankly, this information is gold dust. You can find it at: www.economist.com/mediadirectory

- Approach the journalist with something that will pique their intellectual curiosity or that plays to areas that will interest them (remembering that they are writing for an international, elite audience).

- While they may well respond quickly if they are interested, don't expect them to jump on it immediately unless it is to do with something they are actively writing that week. Don't be surprised if they also say: "That is really interesting, can you come back in four months as I would like to look at it then?"

Getting into the *Harvard Business Review*

Appearing in the *Harvard Business Review* is one of the very pinnacles of thought leadership. It is harder to think of anything that provides greater bragging rights than having been featured here.

It is easier to get in the magazine's blog than into the magazine itself. While the magazine will have bigger impact, being in the blog at least allows you to say: "As I said in the *Harvard Business Review* recently..."

In fact appearing only online is no longer the booby prize it used to be. If your online article features in social media, or prominently in an email from a publication to its subscribers, it can still get a huge amount of attention.

There isn't any secret about getting into the *HBR*, here is what you do:

- Buy it, read it, study it (print and online).

- There's no need for guesswork as to what they're looking for. The *Harvard Business Review* gives detailed guidelines on their requirements and how to submit ideas at http://hbr.org/guidelines-for-authors-hbr (this is well worth reading even if you aren't looking for coverage in the *HBR*; it contains great advice and this applies equally to any thought leadership you produce).

- Design your thought leadership right from the start so that it meets the *HBR*'s stringent requirements. The more big global brands it relates to, the better, so make especially sure this is designed in from the start (the *HBR* is seeking to get more articles aimed at mid-market and high-growth technology businesses, so be aware of this too).

- For an interview with the current *HBR* editor giving useful colour about the magazine and his editorial goals, go to www.kelsopr.com/thought-leadership-manual-resources

Getting on reality TV

Once upon a time the world of business was largely ignored by broadcasters as a source of entertainment.

This is no longer the case and over the past 20 years or so there has been a huge change, driven by the rise of reality TV, the expansion in the number of channels and also entrepreneurialism becoming much more sexy and aspirational.

Trail blazers like Sir John Harvey-Jones (BBC's original *Troubleshooter*) and series such as *Trouble at the Top* have been followed by all manner of memorable and not-so-memorable shows.

If getting in the *HBR* is hard, getting on to mainstream TV is even harder – but all manner of people have managed it, from undertakers (FA Albin & Sons – *Don't Drop the Coffin*) and call centre providers (Save Britain Money Ltd – *The Call Centre*) to behavioural change consultants (Seven Suphi – *The Naked Office*).

In fact, whether you are the star of the show or on the receiving end of advice, the huge impact of being on mainstream television invariably causes a dramatic boost in sales for any business (as well as bringing television celebrity stardust to those who appear).

What are the options for featuring on a TV show?

Now, for most people being on a business reality TV show is not for them or their business, but for a few it is very achievable. Television channels know that business formats can work, and that some business people are able to become television personalities.

Think you'd like to be on a TV show? Here's how to do it...

There are effectively three ways that you can appear in a business TV reality show:

1 - Be the star of your own series

Here the series directly revolves around you handing out advice to other businesses or individuals.

Here the key requirement is generally a strong and colourful personality for the star, who dispenses no-nonsense advice in memorable and entertaining ways.

Examples include: *The Troubleshooter; Ramsay's Kitchen Nightmares; The Fairy Jobmother; Badger or Bust; The Call Centre; The Hotel Inspector; Dickinson's Real Deal;* all sorts of property makeover shows; *Beat the Boss; The Naked Office.* Not seen some of them? Look them up on Google for more info and back episodes.

2 - Your business is the star

Here the series notionally is about your business, although in reality your business is a central nexus around which lots of stories about customers, employees and others are explored.

Examples include: *The Dog Hotel* (about a new pooch grooming parlour); *The Auction House; Luton Airport; Can't Pay? We'll Take It Away!* (bailiffs); *A Life of Grime* (council environmental health inspectors); *Eddie Stobart: Trucks & Trailers; The Museum* (life at the British Museum); *Don't Drop the Coffin.*

3 - Be featured in an existing format

Here you appear as a one-off, either with you or your business being profiled, or on the receiving end of advice.

Examples of the former include: *Undercover Boss; Secret Millionaire; Dragons' Den; Trouble at the Top.*

Examples where businesses and their owners are on the receiving end of advice from gurus include: *The Troubleshooter; The Naked Office; Ramsay's Kitchen Nightmares; The Hotel Inspector; Badger or Bust.*

Business reality shows appear on all sorts of channels – not just the five main terrestrial ones but also Sky and various digital channels.

Being on television, particularly primetime shows like those above, has a huge impact. For instance, *Undercover Boss* gets two to three million viewers per episode on Channel 4, while shows on BBC and ITV will get more. The huge impact created by TV will raise your personal and business brand in a way other media can't.

Willard Foxton of television production company Pioneer Productions advises:

1. Have a good look at other business reality shows; see how they work and what the elements are that bring on the drama, necessary for entertaining TV.

2. Think clearly how this would work for your business.

3. Have a really clear business objective for doing it; for instance, do you want to boost sales, be seen as a really great place to work, or maybe you want to alter aspects of your reputation? Don't go in with woolly objectives like 'wouldn't it be great for us to be on TV!'

4. While you can approach TV channels directly, for most businesses it is best to work with a TV production company that has lots of experience doing business reality TV shows. The way to find them is to think of reality shows that are sort

of similar to what you have in mind, then track down the production company behind them on the internet.

5. The key person is the head of development. Email them with your proposal, pressing relevant buttons about the variety of human drama and entertainment opportunities that will arise from your proposal.

6. Be persistent and keep following up until you get an answer. If you get knocked back, don't give up (maybe the idea isn't exciting to them or maybe it is a great idea but they simply can't commission it at that moment for all sorts of reasons).

Always bear in mind that these companies are run by disorganised creatives, so you very much need to make the running and be persistent.

Once you have got a production company on side, the next stage is typically a pilot show. The production company may commission this themselves, but more likely they will first seek a channel to back it, which can take a considerable amount of time.

If the pilot show is a success, this will lead to a first series.

Editorial control?

Do not expect to have any editorial control; the production company will not allow you to decide what goes in and what goes out once filming begins.

The control you exercise is right at the start by determining what areas and people they have access to.

This needs to be clearly agreed with them well in advance, and you need to be clear on any elements you cannot deliver (eg if you have a certain type of client who absolutely will never agree to take part, then this needs to be clear at the start. Another example is if you are not going to allow access to certain locations or at certain times).

The power of television

By way of illustrating the dramatic impact appearing on television in a mainstream show can have, according to Studio Lambert, the company that produces *Undercover Boss*:

* Each series has rated highly on Channel 4, commanding audiences in excess of two million.

* The *Financial Times* ran a piece in December 2010 about *Undercover Boss* being the most effective way a company can improve public opinion of its brand.

* According to Google Trends, after episodes of *Undercover Boss* air, the organisation featured that evening consistently appears as a Top 10 search on Google.

* After taking part in the series:

  • Ann Summers reported that online customer acquisitions went up 351% after broadcast.

  • The enquiry rate in business at Isuzu Trucks increased by 500%.

  • The animal charity Blue Cross's website crashed with the weight of online donations being made.

Isn't there a danger they will stitch us up and we'll look foolish?

People often worry that the lighthearted side of television and the need to entertain will mean they are being set up for a lampooning.

Willard Foxton says: "99% of the time there is absolutely no intention to stitch up businesses. However, if something dramatic happens, or things go wrong spectacularly, then this is great TV and they will include it.

"Similarly, if you put forward people for interviews, whether employees or customers, and they say outrageous or controversial things, then the company will include it. If they're filming your Christmas party and a drunken fight breaks out, it will go in.

"These sorts of dramatic incidents are what are technically known in the TV business as 'the best bits'! So it's not so much a case of not being stitched up, it is more a case of don't provide the rope that you will hang yourself with.

"A great example of this is *The Call Centre*, where the filming captured various breaches of data regulations and making nuisance calls, so the company received a £225,000 fine. Clearly, if you are doing something questionable, prevent that area being filmed or sort it out beforehand!

"On the very rare occasions that a production company is looking to make a business look ridiculous, the first tell-tale sign is that the description of the format will have a giveaway phrase like 'This is a lighthearted show'.

"Also, always find out who is the proposed presenter. Another warning sign of a potential stitch-up is having a presenter who is largely known for stand-up comedy... although this isn't always the case, as we've just done a show with a stand-up doing his first serious voice-over work. So, if you are worried about it not being the right place for your company, do your homework and thorough background research."

SECTION V
FROM GOOD TO *GREAT*: MAKING YOUR THOUGHT LEADERSHIP THE VERY BEST IT CAN BE

CHAPTER 17

The biggest secret for successful thought leadership

OK, this chapter makes a big promise. Maybe what I am going to reveal may seem more like common sense than a secret, but given the number of firms that fail to do it, it certainly isn't widely appreciated at all.

The secret for being a successful thought leader is: Repetition!

Repetition... Repetition...

Once something works really well, repeat it!

One-off initiatives often work well, but the most successful ones are those that are designed to be repeated periodically – whether quarterly, half-yearly or annually. Examples are varied and include:

- The CBI's monthly business confidence index (which not only makes news headlines but is also widely referred to by the City and policy makers).

- Several of the thought leadership examples case studied in this book, including: *The Deloitte Annual Review of Football Finance*; KPMG's *Fraud Barometer*; and the GlobalExpense Employee Expenses Benchmark report.

- 'Woodstock for Capitalists' is the nickname for the annual general meeting of American conglomerate Berkshire Hathaway Inc. Each year it fills a stadium with about 38,000 shareholders from around the world attending to hear Warren Buffett and Charlie Munger talk about the company, the economy, and their investment philosophy. Neither their investment style nor their approach to the meetings has changed much since the 1970s, when only a dozen people would typically attend: it's the same formula of them discussing their investment wisdom, delivered with a Midwestern homespun feel, coupled with boringly regular high investment returns.

Having thought leadership initiatives that are repeatable makes your life much easier.

Rather than constantly seeking ideas and sourcing data, you can concentrate on making a tested methodology work better.

On top of this come huge marketing advantages (see the boxed section about why repeatability is important) and, best of all, if you have a repeatable process, once it is up and running you can delegate a lot of the work to others!

Why is repeatability important?

- You develop valuable know-how that ensures you get better each time you repeat it.

- You aren't constantly wasting effort creating basic infrastructure – you can build on your past experience and investments.

- It very firmly keeps you up to date with what is happening in the market, and embodies this to clients and prospects.

- It becomes an established event and people start to expect it and request it.

- It takes sustained activity over a long period if you're going to make an impression on people who don't already know you – repeatable initiatives deliver this.

- You become known for the initiative, strongly positioning you as 'part of the industry'.

- If something is repeatable, you can create systems and processes to delegate much of the work to someone else once it is up and running.

- You build up all-important trend data, which is not only much more newsworthy, it also gives you greater insights and stronger thought leadership.

How do you build in repeatability?

If you are going to build in repeatability to a research initiative you need to use data that is updated periodically, whether through surveys, benchmarking or other means.

Also, choosing an area where things change is clearly helpful for making your reports interesting.

However, many sectors aren't like that. Often the changes are more glacial, with one period's data looking not dissimilar to the previous period. How do you overcome the lack of change giving few new angles?

One way is to focus particularly on different aspects each time. So in year one, you might look at one area in more detail, in the second year you might include the same core areas but pay particular attention to another area (preferably one where you think there is something topical or attention-grabbing happening).

If you can't create an initiative that can be repeated, then at the very least stick with the same industry or topic so you have a programme of regular initiatives (white papers, events, etc).

Don't fall into the trap that catches out many firms who spread their resources too thinly. Some even deliberately do not repeat successful initiatives on the basis "John's initiative went really well last year, so this year we won't support it and instead we will put the resources behind another department so someone else gets a turn".

Logical, but disastrous: if something was successful the first time, it should be even more successful the next time – so keep backing it!

CHAPTER 18

Involving clients in your thought leadership

Many businesses have a one-dimensional view on how they involve their clients in their thought leadership: they send it to them once it is completed and use it to try to sell additional projects.

This is great, but it is very different from the "we work in a partnership with our clients" that many businesses claim; the buyer/seller relationship is not a partnership.

While many firms feel the right way to deliver thought leadership is with a surprise raid, like the Japanese at Pearl Harbour (or perhaps it should be like the British at Battle of Taranto if you want an example on the right side), with their emails swooping in at dawn, out of the blue, intended to deliver a knockout blow with PDF torpedoes. I'd strongly urge you to think differently!

Thought leadership projects are great opportunities to actually do something in partnership with clients – something that's not selling and not chargeable hours.

Instead, think of orchestrating your campaign as an escalation of activity, with the publishing of the report being a high point in a campaign that started well in advance, and finishes long after.

The benefits of involving clients in your project as it develops include:

- They will bring a different perspective and first-hand knowledge.

- They can provide additional resources.

- Involving them as a case study, or at least as an endorsement.

- Getting them to speak at your events and appear in the report.

- Giving you greater confidence that the insights and conclusions will genuinely grab the interest of people involved in it on a daily basis.

Ways of involving select clients early in your thought leadership include:

- Discussions at an early stage about the initiative's theme (whether one-to-one or through having a discussion dinner and subtly using it as a focus group to gauge areas of particular interest, gain insights and provoke fresh perspectives).

- Research involving clients, whether quantitative (an opinion poll) or qualitative (detailed and thoughtful questioning to gaining insights and capturing the nuances of particular perspectives and situations).

- Joint projects. These can take all sorts of forms with examples including:

    ○ Involving a small number of people from clients with particular interest in the subject in some sort of steering or consultative role

- ○ With bigger clients, there may be many ways to use their data, customers or employees within the research
- Including them in the peer review of your themes and conclusions.

CHAPTER 19

Writing like a thought leader

In this book we have shared global best practice that your business can leverage to ensure thought leadership synergises with your existing core competencies. You'll be able to use it with c-suite decision makers to create a burning platform that, combined with outside-the-box thinking, provides a robust and holistic solution that reveals their critical paradigms.

Clearly it's nonsense, yet there is nothing in this that isn't in widespread use in outpourings from would-be thought leaders.

Indeed, if crimes against the English language were punishable offences, our prisons would be full of professionals and technologists with great school results, degrees and long track records of writing essays and reports.

So, what is the correct style of writing to influence people?

Authoritative, yes. Boring, no. If you are to influence, you need to be understood.

That requires both clarity of thought and clarity of expression, not ideas that have been dressed up in long words and complex sentences.

Former Touche Ross partner Gerry Boon (case studied on page 28 for his hugely successful thought leadership that created its sector-leading Sports Business Group), says: "My maxim was always 'write as you would speak'. That will automatically help you avoid jargon as well as provide clarity by keeping you to short sentences."

It's great advice, and echoes my own approach to this book where I have tried my best to capture my own voice in the wording. This tone may not be to everyone's preference, but it is authentic and distinctively mine.

Ditch the jargon

Don't be afraid to ditch the jargon! Using it fools no one, except the gullible.

The people who get invited to speak on television, conference platforms, seminars and in boardrooms are those who make their points clearly, succinctly and in a manner people quickly understand.

Jargon achieves none of this – in fact it obfuscates.

Whether you want to adopt a conversational tone is a matter of preference, but it is well worth noting that *The Economist* takes the same approach with its leader columns at the start of the magazine – as does Warren Buffett, the world's most successful investor.

Either way, whatever tone you adopt, the keys to communicating your ideas successfully are:

- Express your ideas clearly
- Express them memorably, which includes making them interesting
- Express them in a way that people who aren't experts will understand

We have already explored how to talk about your findings in an interesting way in Chapter 12. Here are a few rules of thumb to check if you and your team have applied this successfully in your writing:

- Avoid long sentences. If a sentence is long it is probably unclear – you most likely should break it up.

- Avoid lots of qualifications and double negatives. If a sentence has lots of commas and qualifications, it is probably unclear – you should break it up.

- If you are using clichés and business jargon you could well be masking sloppy thinking, so remove them. If they aren't masking slopping thinking, remove them anyway!

- Can your writing be easily understood by someone who is reasonably intelligent but knows nothing about the subject – say a 17-year-old student? If not, rewrite it so it can be widely understood.

What if my writing is genuinely awful?

Being always able to write in clear punchy English is something that takes journalists many years to master, so it is not surprising that many people find it difficult.

Turgid prose is going to be hard work for your audience, and many of them are not going to want to spend their time wading through convoluted sentences.

If writing is a problem for you, the main thing to do is to recognise this and work around it. Options include:

- Write it, and give someone a free hand to rewrite it – but don't just dump it on the poor old marketing team, get a professional sub-editor to do it. People don't appreciate the difference that having a document professionally edited makes until they experience it.

- Don't write it. Instead dictate, and get someone to transcribe it.

- Get a ghost-writer (someone who will interview you and draft it).

- Deliver it verbally through podcasts or video.

There are also lots of books on how to be a better writer – it is well worth investing in one, but they aren't magic wands. You have to put in the effort. If you are in a hurry to finish the report, consider whether you also have the time to train your writing skills simultaneously, or if this is a job for another occasion.

Concluding comments

Job vacancy: thought leader with interesting insights

We've covered a lot of areas in this book. After all, the creation and execution of a thought leadership campaign requires many skills: knowledge; creativity; project management; persuasion; discipline; writing; and a wide range of business development skills too.

You will have realised that successful modern marketing and sales, for businesses with high-value services, requires the generation of a regular flow of attention-grabbing ideas.

After all, without these what are your PR, social media, blog and presentations going to draw on? Where is the intellectual content for your 'content marketing' strategy going to appear from? If you are going to adopt 'challenger selling' with your prospects, where is the knowledge and confidence to deliver that challenge going to come from?

Some firms will continue with the old ways of me-centred marketing, pushing their features and capabilities and how they are so much better than their competitors (when really they are pretty indistinguishable).

It's not that this won't work all the time, just that it certainly won't work when the firm faces a team that is genuinely an expert in this area; one that displays the passion, knowledge and commercial insights that clients really want from their advisers.

Most firms have a big vacancy for the sort of people who can deliver this. The role won't be advertised and its need may not even be recognised – but it will be there nonetheless and will be waiting for someone with drive to seize it.

Good luck, and I hope this book provides you and your firm with useful tools that will help you become even more successful.

How Kelso Consulting can help you deliver great thought leadership

I very much hope this book has inspired you to create fantastic results for your business through thought leadership campaigns that create great insights and lots of clients too.

If you are looking for additional support, the team at Kelso Consulting provide the following support for thought leadership campaigns:

- Working with you throughout to create and deliver a successful campaign

- Specific support at particular times through our Thought Leadership Bootcamp programme, including:

  ◦ Creating the business case

  ◦ Facilitating your creation of breakthrough ideas

  ◦ Helping you deliver the maximum sales 'bang for the buck'

For more information about how Kelso Consulting can help your business GRAB the attention of your clients with great ideas, please contact us on +44(0)20 7242 2286 or see further details on www.kelsopr.com/thought-leadership-manual-resources

Acknowledgements:

I'd particularly like to acknowledge the people who have given me such a wide range of help with creating this book, which has occupied a large chunk of the past year.

Initially, I dawdled about for a couple of years in creating a book, getting nowhere. Things changed when I went on The Book Midwife programme – a big thanks to Mindy and Kate for enabling me to make it happen, and for providing lots of support and great advice along the way.

Other support included my brother Steven, who produced the graphics in the book as well as carefully proofreading much of my initial manuscript, and Vicky Palumbo for typing up my rambling dictation.

I am very grateful to the following interviewees for providing their valuable time and excellent insights:

Stephen Blundell, Redstone Consultants

Gerry Boon, chairman of Matchchat and sports business consultant

Ian Brodie, marketing guru for freelance consultants

Terry Corby, marketing and strategy consultant

Willard Foxton, Pioneer Productions

Kate Gibbons, Clifford Chance

Simon James, Clifford Chance

Sarah Reavley, Remark

Peter Thomas, Accenture

I am also very grateful to the following people who generously took time to review the book and gave valuable feedback, improving the book no end:

Stephen Blundell, Redstone Consultants

Gerry Boon, chairman of Matchchat and sports business consultant

Des Greene, Saffery Champness

Robert Pay, Alvarez & Marsal

Alex Powell, EY

Sarah Reavley, Remark

Charlie King, Emma Ramsay and Anna Ryland at Kelso Consulting

A thanks also to Chris Matthews of SutherlandsPugh for inspiring the approach of pages 76 and 77, and to to The Bloom Group whose ideas helped significantly in the factors listed on page 174.

I'd also like very much to thank my family for putting up with me being locked away in my study for far too many evenings and weekends in 2014 working on the book!

Further reading and resources:

- **Workbook of tables and self-assessments** – available on the resources webpage

- **List of further reading** – available on the resources webpage

- **List of useful online data resources** – available on the resources webpage

These and other useful material, only available to readers of The Thought Leadership Manual, are available at www.kelsopr.com/thought-leadership-manual-resources

About the author

Tim Prizeman is the owner of public relations and thought leadership agency Kelso Consulting, and the book builds on his experiences of working with numerous professional and technology firms over the past 17 years to devise and implement successful initiatives.

He and his team advise businesses of all sizes, particularly consultancy, professional and business technology firms that provide high-value services and need strong relationships with directors, owners and senior decision makers.

Previously he worked in-house in senior PR roles with two of the world's largest accountancy and consultancy firms.

Tim has won various national PR and marketing awards for campaigns he has devised and delivered for his clients, several of which have gone on to become his clients' main annual lead-development initiatives.

His interests include martial arts and, when time permits, snow-boarding – but he has resisted the urge to include any tenuous metaphors relating to these!

Manufactured by Amazon.ca
Bolton, ON